The Hour Is Now

Franz Cardinal König

The Hour Is Now

Translated by
Herbert W. Richardson

Harper & Row, Publishers
New York, Evanston,
San Francisco, London

 For information address Harper & Row, Publishers, Inc., 10 East 53rd Street, New York, N.Y. 10022. Published simultaneously in Canada by Fitzhenry & Whiteside Limited, Toronto.

FIRST EDITION

Designed by Janice Stern

Library of Congress Cataloging in Publication Data
König, Franz, Cardinal, 1905–
The hour is now.

Translation of Die Stunde der Welt.
1. Meditations. I. Title.
BX2184.K6313 1975 242 74–4642
ISBN 0–06–064772–8

Translator's Preface

Last spring this little book came, as if by mere accident, into my hands. But it was one of those "accidents" that seem to be mysteriously arranged. I opened the book at random and read several paragraphs. They described so perfectly how I felt, and guided my inner thoughts so helpfully, that I was excited—and grateful. The passage was discussing suffering. I turned to another, a description of the spiritual life. I was not disappointed. I read then with great joy a whole chapter on how to believe in Jesus Christ, and another on the variety of tasks and gifts within the church.

As I read, something within me confirmed the truth of the writer's words—and I could sense the love in his heart. Most of all, however, I responded to the wisdom of the author. Here was a man who thought with his head, loved with his heart, and added to both the accumulated wisdom of many years of life and diverse experience. So I was helped by him, as by a wise father and counselor.

In my enthusiasm, I started to translate the book from its original German into English. I wanted not merely to put down English words that would be equivalent to German words, but to translate the wisdom and love and help that I had found there. Could I make my translation not merely saying the words of Father König over again, but something that would also include my own sense of their truth and importance? That is what this exercise has meant to me.

To me, this little book is a beautiful blending of the catholic love for values wherever they are found and the evangelical passion for Jesus Christ and his power to transform the human heart. I can find no better way to commend it to the reader than by this public expression of my personal gratitude to the author.

Herbert Richardson
St. Michael's College, Toronto
July 3, 1974

Contents

The Hour Is Now

1. The Great Longing of Faith

A great longing fills our hearts. We wait impatiently for something that has not yet appeared. We have so much already—all kinds of pleasure to choose from, more than we could ever need. Yet we are restless and uneasy. We still search frantically for happiness. We still want something that is real. The very people who seem to have everything are the ones most filled with a great longing. What do we want?

In spite of our high standard of living, we see how personal conflicts and difficulties increase on every side. We hear about the rapid increase of human neurosis in our society. Some of us turn to psychiatrists for our cure; others turn to drugs. What do people want? What is still lacking? What makes us today so psychologically sick that tomorrow even our bodies will become ill?

Our Deepest Question

Someone once described religion as the answer to our search for meaning. Perhaps this is the root of our problem today. A kind of "practical atheism" exists everywhere in the world today. This practical atheism is not limited only to the United States. It is found also in Europe, Africa, and Asia. But this atheism can give only superficial answers to man's deepest questions. In fact, it even creates a whole set of new problems. Our deepest question is this: What meaning does life really have? Everywhere in the world today one discovers a driving need to find answers. What is life all about? What's the point to everything? Why am I here on this earth? Is it nonsense to ask these questions? Is it even crazy?

Of course, people don't ask these questions all the

time. For long periods, people live simply and directly, without wondering about the ultimate meaning of things. People work and eat; they are happy and hopeful; they go to bed and get up. And through all this the meaning of life seems to be obvious and secure. But sooner or later the question begins to take shape: Is this all there is to life? The question becomes more urgent when we begin to lose the things for which we have lived: when a baby dies, when someone we love becomes incurably ill, when we feel our own decreased vitality and sense the inevitability of death. In such moments we say to ourselves, "My life is just falling to pieces." Yet sometimes we begin to feel life is meaningless when we are right at the peak of things. For example, a man may have worked and established a successful business. He now has everything he has always wanted. Suddenly, right at this moment, he says to himself, "Why am I in this rat race anyway? Run, run, run—day in and day out. What for?" In a moment like this, a man begins to feel that all his life and work is shallow and empty.

And so we begin to reflect. Everyone has to die someday, and everything else has to pass away: all that we own, all our pleasures, those happy moments, the things we've created with our hands. What, then, is the purpose of it all? Oh, of course, we comfort ourselves by saying, "I'm living for my children," or "I'm living to make a contribution to society. We feel that by making our own small contribution, we help to keep the whole process of human life going. But the question still nags us: What is this whole process of human life all about? Why is it here and where is it going? And this question can become sharper and more pointed, like a knife—for when we ourselves are afflicted by suffering we wonder, "Why go on living in pain and torture? Why keep struggling to stay alive?"

The Discovery of Meaning

But there are times when we have quite different kinds of experience. There are days when we not only experience things to be meaningful, but when something ultimate and complete lives in us so that we know and believe it directly. It may be in the certainty that we have found a true friend. It may be something we discover in our children or in our work. Or, for some, this experience of ultimate meaning may come when we discover for the first time that we can really be of help to others and are really needed. In moments like this we know there is meaning. No further questions arise and no further explanations are needed.

In such moments, a person experiences something absolute. He may not be able to explain exactly what he experiences. He may only describe how he feels about it. Whenever we experience something as unconditionally meaningful in this way, what we experience is a fulfillment, an ultimate value.

Moreover, when we experience something of this sort, then we know it is important. We can never again treat it as trivial. We know that this—whatever it is—is worthwhile; and we know that we have some kind of responsibility toward it. We feel a sense of obligation to it, feel there are things that we should seek to do. If, for some reason, we can't do or be what we feel called to do or be, then we feel guilty. It's impossible to explain why we feel all these things, but we know about them from our own experience. We know that whenever we experience something as ultimately meaningful, then we regard it as important and treat it as worthwhile. Why? We don't know why, but we know it's true. It's not a matter of science, but of conscience. Not by arguments do we know these things about life's meaning, but by some inner insight or conviction. Whenever someone has come to this conviction by his own experience, it is his forever and no one can take it away.

Primal Faith

The innermost certainty that human beings have about what is absolutely meaningful is faith, the primal faith of a person. No one can prove it, but also no one can take it away—for it arises out of everyone's own innermost experience. That is why we believe as we do even when all our friends and acquaintances disagree. This primal faith is also an expression of love. Whatever is experienced as absolutely meaningful is also experienced as worthwhile and valuable. To value something is to love it. The person who feels that he ought to care for and protect something is feeling a love for that thing. Whoever values a person loves that person. And, whoever has experienced anything as absolutely meaningful is also someone who is hopeful. In saying yes to some meaning in life, we are also saying that life should go on and that life's journey does not come to a dead end. This affirmation is a sign of our hope and confidence. Whoever experiences the unconditional meaningfulness of life in this way feels the strength to live which flows from it. He experiences, too, a joy in living. He has an inward certainty that he is going in the right direction.

God as Absolute Meaning

The faith in the "absolutely meaningful" that we experience is always a decision. This decision, if made consciously, occurs in the depths of our heart. Here the Absolute meets us. There's no way to prove it. Anyone can say, "I won't take anything seriously; I won't commit myself to anything; I won't feel responsibility or guilt; I want an easy life." But this easy life would also be a worthless life, a meaningless life, a life that in the last analysis was not conscious of itself.

We ask ourselves, therefore, what this absolute meaning is. We can experience it in so many little things. The world is like a great mosaic, composed of many little pieces. Only when I know how the many little pieces all fit together in a big picture do I understand their meaning and see the sense of the world as whole. An individual person or a single thing is like a small wheel (for example, a little cogwheel) that I might find on the street. By itself it can do nothing. Alone, it has no meaning. Only when it is put together with something with which it belongs does it have a meaning.

If a human life, like any small thing, needs to be a part of a larger context in order to have meaning, then what is the ultimate context, the great whole that is meaningful in itself? Only the absolutely unlimited can have its meaning in itself alone. Since beyond this infinite reality there is nothing else, infinite reality cannot be part of anything else. It is complete in itself. It is where every other journey finds its end. It is the completion of every meaning. It is ultimate meaning. To know this is an inward revelation, a personal illumination, a meeting with the secret of the Absolute.

To know this is grace itself.

A decision about ultimate meaning is similar to the love between two persons. After all the arguments for and against, after all the vacillations, one finally comes to the point of a decision: yes or no. This is a fundamental, enduring, and unwavering decision: a person now believes or else he refuses to believe, just as he accepts or rejects love. We have experienced ultimate meaning. We know in our deepest conscience that we are committed and that we are responsible.

But who can commit me in my innermost being? Who can put demands upon me in the depths of my heart? Or encourage and strengthen me there? This ultimate meaning, this unlimited demand that has met me in the midst of my life can be neither human nor less than human. What is human is not absolute. What is human is not that total something that can put a total demand on my life. On the other hand, this absolute meaning must be something personal. It cannot be less than we are because it engages us inwardly with an absolute demand. So we believe in that reality which for thousands of years all people have called by the name of "God": the unlimited, the absolute, the personal God who calls us in our deepest heart.

God Meets Us in This World

The absolute meaning: that is God. The ultimate meaning of our lives: that is God. The final purpose of this universe: that is God. But this unlimited, absolute, demanding God meets us in this world. He does not wait only at the end of our life's way, at the end of our journey, at the end of time. He meets us, rather, in every experience of value and meaning that we have. Wherever we have experienced something as unconditionally meaningful—whether a moment, a person, a task, or love—there we are meeting God. God meets us wherever unconditional meaning comes into our lives. God does not exist in some faraway beyond, but encounters us in all the things we value in this world. The way the Bible says this is, "Wherever someone truly loves and loves without limit, there God is present in him." Wherever there is real love, there God is real, too. Whoever loves abides in God, and love springs from God since God is love itself.

This is the gospel. It tells us about the fulfillment of our lives. It gives them their true completion. It offers a meaning for us to live by. But it is not enough simply to hear the words of the gospel and try to understand these words with the mind alone. The gospel can only be really understood and accepted when it is lived. Only as we live meaningfully will we be able to understand the meaning of life. Only to the extent that we take life and all that belongs to it *seriously* will we understand that reality which is to be taken with absolute seriousness. Only to the extent that we live *responsibly* will we understand the real inward responsibility, the deepest sense of duty and concern. Only to the extent that we live *conscientiously* will we have an inner conscience and self-knowledge. Only to the extent that we recognize the many values of life will we also recognize what is unconditionally valuable. In a word: only as we truly love will God come to us. Whoever denies that there is meaning in life, whoever accepts no responsibility or duty, whoever ignores his conscience: that person can also no longer believe or hope or love. He does not know God.

8

Faith in the Living God is faith in the meaning, purpose, and content of our lives. That is why we say that if the world seeks him today, then it will find peace, joy, inward fulfillment and a meaningful life.

2. The Encounter of Faith

I believe that a secret longing for God is still alive in the hearts of most people. But perhaps it is blocked up because of the restless, noisy rush of our everyday life. Perhaps in earlier times it was different; perhaps then it was easier to believe. But how can a person living in the twentieth century attain to a true and deep faith and become aware again of the deep inner longing for God?

By the year 2000, it is likely that over 80 percent of the world population will be living in big cities. Can we realize what that means? Millions and millions of people will be penned up in little apartments, more cramped together than anywhere today. Where will anyone find a bit of privacy to meditate or pray? Masses of people will tumble through the streets, all having to fulfill their programmed routines of daily work, surrounded on all sides by noise, stimulation, and the press of the restless unthinking crowd. There will be no escape. Wherever you drive there will be long lines of cars filled with people who, like you, are trying to get away to some quiet place, someplace where they can find and be themselves. Do you realize what a situation like this means for faith in God? For hope? For human love?

Faith in the Year 2000

People who lived in earlier times—farmers, small businessmen, villagers—may have worked fourteen or sixteen hours every day. But their age was a more reflective one. Even during the rush of harvest season, a little time for prayer would be set aside. (At least that is the memory of those who can still remember this past time.) People were then often alone with themselves and with God; with nature and with their own thoughts. They could wonder about the why's and whither's of life—where it comes from, what its meaning is, and where it is going. People could meditate and become aware of the mystery of life and its unfathomable secrets. And they could ponder how they should live.

This was a time in which people still could experience God in a special way through prayer. The man of prayer and the mystic were admired and felt to be relevant and committed people. Those who lived in monasteries, praying alone in their cells, were the ones who made known something of the great encounter with God that they themselves had experienced. They could talk about it with others, and others believed them, for their very lives were an evidence for God.

There was true mysticism then. As everything was rooted in God, so also was human life. In the depths of the human heart, the Creator meets his creation. Traditionally, this meeting was called "the little spark, or inward light within the soul." So as soon as a person came to himself, he also came to God. Faith in God was rooted more deeply in the hearts of those who attained to a deeper awareness of themselves and, therefore, also of God. This was an age of faith, even though there was human sin just as today. But people knew about God. And when they lay on their deathbed, they still asked for a priest. They *believed* in God.

Can we now understand what it means that by the year 2000 practically everyone will live in big cities? What it means that no one will have any privacy to be alone with God? What it means that there will be no quiet place where a person can be alone with God in order to have a direct experience of him? Can we understand, now, why there is such a great crisis about faith in God? Can we appreciate why Teilhard de Chardin speaks of the "terrifying impact of an irresistibly expanding atheism"? Can we grasp why it is that of all human questions, the question, "Are we totally alone in this universe?" hangs like a shadow over all the others? Pope Paul has reminded us that "vis-à-vis world atheism, we have to remain faithful today." But the decision concerning faith in God won't be decided by writing clever books that analyze all the problems concerning God and debate them pro and con. The decision concerning faith in God will be decided by our being or not being able to experience God—even in the year 2000! We have to find a way so this can happen. That's our present problem. Even a person living in the twenty-first century will have to worry about how to come to God through prayer. In spite of all difficulties he will have to create a time for a turning inward, for quietness, for reflection and increased awareness. It will be harder for him than for his parents. But such prayer will no longer be sufficient to give him an adequate experience of God. In our time, God is urging us to encounter him not only in prayer, but also in other ways. In years to come, the quietness of prayer will be even more threatened than it is today. If we can no longer then meet and experience God in prayer, then faith in God will be even more threatened and undermined than now. For this reason, in the future we must seek to encounter God in the midst of our human encounters. Far more than in the past, we must meet God through our meeting one another. Jesus Christ himself has already said to us: "Whatever you've done to the least of my brothers, you've also done it to me." Since every person is rooted in God, God can meet us when we encounter one another.

God in Our Fellowman

Some might now ask: "How is it that God is to be encountered in our fellowman?" To begin with, we have the impression that other people have nothing whatsoever to do with God. We meet so many others. We sigh, saying, we can't concern ourselves about them all—we have to get on with our lives. Even when someone is lying on the sidewalk or has had an accident on the street, the swarm of people pass by without concern, except, perhaps, for a moment's curiosity. Many wonder how anyone can manage to worry about all the poverty and wretchedness in this world. Our fellowman is most often merely a stranger to us —a shadow person, a number, a mere nobody-at-all. Even when we worry about our fellowman, we do it mainly because he is useful to us because of the work he does. We need other people for their labor, sometimes for their company; but we don't need them for themselves alone.

We have, of course, some more delightful experiences with other people. Sometimes we have good companions; sometimes we have good friends. We can feel very close to our father and mother. There is real love among people, and a few people do mean a great deal to us. We feel dutybound to these persons whom we love. We feel responsible for them—and not just because we've been told to be so. Rather, some inner wisdom makes us know we owe them faithfulness, openness, concern, and respect. And if we fail to be this way with them, we then carry within us a little sense of guilt.

We feel the people we love are important. Whatever happens to them happens also to us. Whatever happens to them is important and meaningful to us as well; it gets to us. Alongside these people we feel at home, happy, satisfied. To be near them is to be at peace. Their friendship and love seem to us to be unconditionally meaningful. A certain life-giving power flows from these relationships, and they cannot and must not be torn asunder.

Let us ask ourselves now just what in our relation to these people we love binds us to them in our innermost selves and demands something from us. Why is it unthinkable to say that I could be faithless, unconcerned, unkind, and irresponsible towards them? Where does this inner conscience that tells us that we ought to feel or do something for them come from? If we're really honest about it, we must confess that only something Absolute is able to bind and hold us in this absolute way. Only the Lord of Life can put demands like this in our heart of hearts. Only a personal God can urge me to this kind of inward responsibility, for he alone can require me to give answer and he alone can know the secrets of my heart.

Deciding to Believe

A person might have to struggle to gain this insight, especially since so many around us think differently. One is always tempted to say, "Why should someone else really concern me?" One is tempted to withdraw and keep other people at a distance. The decision is never easy. No one can force us one way or the other.

The decision can go either way and we make it freely. But in the depths of himself, no one can escape the feeling that he has responsibility. I simply can't believe it's true that I can just take or leave a person I love—howsoever *I* prefer it. That way of living wouldn't be really human. It would be an insensitive life: unkind, unconcerned, faithless. It would be a worthless, meaningless, loveless life—a life that was totally false.

So one day a decision must be made. We must say, "Yes, I believe that in my relation with this other person something important is at stake, some true value is presenting itself to me." Such a decision is never arbitrary. In the love for a person that one cares about, the Unconditional itself presents itself to us. In the love for a person to whom one feels oneself absolutely obligated, the Absolute comes to meet us. The Infinite encounters us in and through this person. The Mysterious One, the Infinite God, comes to us in this way. This encounter is a presence of God in the innermost heart, and illumination in the depths of our soul, a pure grace. And in this way we begin to understand the words of Jesus Christ: "Whatsoever you have done to the least of my brothers, you have done it also to me." Wherever we truly love other people, we meet the Lord our God.

Can we begin to understand how much such encounters can be for us a source of strength and of experience of God? They mean much for our faith. We cannot be satisfied only to search for God in the quietness of prayer and in the times we set aside for meditation. We cannot be satisfied to do only as our parents did. Rather, we must get on with searching for God in our relationships with other people. We must do this because if we cannot experience God's presence there, then we cannot believe in God anymore, nor love him, nor hope in him. In the future, the way that Christians approach their fellow human beings will also be the way that they draw near to God.

But understand. We're not talking about a theory here, but about actual deeds of genuine love. We will have to experience anew the truth of the Bible's words: "Whoever abides in love also abides in God" because "God is love." And if we really know this by experience, then we will also begin to understand why the very first page of the Bible speaks of our being "made in the image of God": in the face of every person we see the countenance of God. "Whoever does not love his brother whom he sees cannot love God, who cannot be seen." Today God is demanding that we understand this teaching. He is driving us to the point where either we love our brothers and sisters and come at the same time to experience him—or refuse to love them and, as consequence, experience the breaking down of all our faith.

The love that is tested by the strains of everyday life is the hardest of all, more difficult perhaps than even the sacrifice of martyrdom. It is hard to love the neighbor who plays his radio so impossibly loud late in the evening. It is hard to love the neurotic, intolerably nervous people alongside whom we must work at the office. It is hard to live together in overcrowded apartments with people we simply must bear, and with never a moment's quiet, disturbed constantly by others. Somehow, in the midst of all this, we must find a way to be helpful and loving.

Perhaps we've made too little of such matters in the past. Perhaps we have wanted only that God come to us, give us his grace, and heal our wounds. But today, we must understand that although God still comes to us, he also is calling us to come to him. And he won't come to us if we won't go to him. His coming to us means this: he stirs us up in the depths of our hearts to go to him.

3. Suffering and Faith

Suffering is a part of human life. Weariness, old age, sickness, death, fear of failure, uncertainty, boredom, and obligations that outrun our strength: these are all part of life and come as naturally as the changing of day into night. But there is always that moment when suffering begins to eat itself right into our very bones. Then suffering is not just a part of our life, but life itself. In that moment, life is suffering. In that moment, we are wounded and struck down at the very heart of our being.

The Many Faces of Suffering

What is it that really gets to us and wears us down in this way? Perhaps it is the fear. If someone discovers that he can't keep up with the pace of life either because he is just plain weary or because others simply have more energy, then something inside him begins to rebel as he contemplates the awful fate that may soon befall him. Something inside him struggles against being trodden down or pushed aside when he cannot keep up with others.

Or perhaps what most oppresses us is a feeling that our own lives really aren't worth anything. Our younger years are filled with hope, but later in life we begin to ask ourselves, "Of what importance am I to anyone else? Who is really concerned about me?" We begin, at such times, to sense that we are being shunted to the sidelines of society; we are being pushed out of the spotlight and into the shadows. Who needs us then? Who worries about us? Who is even interested? Something within us rebels against this fate. We resist being treated like a number that can be simply erased from the list of the living. And we refuse to be treated as if we were nothing. Am I really worthless? How can I accept that!

For someone else, the deepest suffering may be sheer loneliness. Like a leaf that has fallen from its tree, this person is cut off and isolated. But when a leaf has fallen from its tree, it cannot go on living. Who doesn't know that? It's the same way with me when I am separated from my whole world. Isn't there anybody who really needs me? Does nobody understand me? Am I simply repudiated and excommunicated by my society? This is what it would feel like to have to live forever all alone.

And then there are apparently trivial occasions that cause people to suffer so, to suffer even unto death. A trivial thing can be the straw that breaks the camel's back. A trivial occasion can become the drop that fills the cup to overflowing, and I simply break down. I can't manage things any longer; I'm at the end of my rope; I can't decide which way to turn. I'm exhausted, helpless, defenseless, useless. Unloved. Cast off. Forgotten. In the end, a person abandons all hope because he doubts that life has a meaning.

Our Greater Life

If suffering has finally touched the very center of one's life in this way, then something decisive begins to happen. Something in a person begins to ripen and mature. One is through, then, with trivia and banality. All the loafing is now over, all the living just to slip by. No more living a superficial life and keeping up with the Joneses. If suffering has finally touched life's very nerve, then life itself cries out inside us. It's all we can think of or feel. It's written before us in great capital letters: LIFE! L I F E ! ! That real life, that worthwhile life, that greater life which must never perish or slip away.

In this situation, a person experiences his own life as really valuable. Even if it is despised and crushed underfoot by others, he still experiences it as real and worthwhile. He knows that it is important and meaningful. He knows he is responsible for it. He knows now that it isn't a matter of indifference whether he just gives up or perseveres. He now can say, "I have a job to do in relation to life—in relation to *my own life.*"

When his innermost self cries this way, a person discovers for the very first time his *own,* his *real,* his *greater* life. Now he really knows what this is. Nothing else could have taught him this—no book, no teacher, no friend. He knows it now from within himself; he knows about this meaningful, important, worthwhile, truly real, greater life. This is an inner certainty that nothing else can give and nothing at all can take away. It is a new consciousness, a *conscience* makes him feel responsible to this greater life. It is as if he had been given life anew, a life for which he must give an accounting.

From out of the labor pains that accompany the suffering unto death, a new life is born. In that moment, a person experiences loss and yet also discovers the greater life. He spontaneously lifts up his eyes to the heavens and says, "Help me, O Lord." Why does he say this? Because he knows, without thinking, that he can't hold onto this greater life by himself. He can't preserve it from death or protect it against danger. It has to be preserved, protected, and brought to fulfillment by some Other. This Other must do more than a human being can do. It must be more than we are. It must be Someone who knows the greater life, the sufferings we bear, and knows how to help us in our pain. Who is it? It is someone more than I am, the one to whom I cry out: "Help me, O Lord."

Where do we get this conviction that the Lord will help us? Why can we, in such moments, believe with such power and say, "Help me, O Lord," with such certainty? We can do this because in such moments we know and even see the greater life. We can do it because we know that this greater life is real and will go on being real. We know that it shall increase in power, come to flower, and shall never die. We know that we shall live, that we shall have greater life. For this reason we trust the one who alone can give us this life in its fullness.

The way of suffering can be a way to God. It is just as real as the way of love, or the way of the quest for truth, or the way of searching for meaning. The way of suffering can affect the heart of a person when he has been struck down in his innermost soul. This is why a person who suffers in this way can be renewed in his heart of hearts: he can be *converted.*

No one can understand this way of suffering unless he has passed along it himself. It's like the way of love: no one can understand how love works unless he loves. For this reason, other people won't understand how it is that someone who has suffered has found, through his suffering, a way to God. No one else can ever fathom what another person has experienced in his innermost depths, in the pit of despair, in the valley of the shadow of death. So some laugh at him. But he knows what he knows.

Job's Lament

Our suffering is not like a television program that we can turn off after we've had enough. Suffering is a bottomless pit: dark, lonely, and frightening. Suffering is that darkness in which Jesus cried out, "My God, my God, why have you left me alone?" Suffering is a kind of darkness that gnaws its way into the inner man so that he is no longer able to see things normally. Where there is real suffering, there is also confusion and inner doubt.

The Old Testament describes the suffering of Job, a believing man who trusted in God alone. The Book of Job tells us how gradually the darkness and the doubt filled his heart:

My life fills me with disgust.
Therefore, I will speak out in the bitterness
of my soul.
I will say to God: Don't damn me like this.

Let me know, at least, why you hate me so.
I am innocent. My life is shattered and my
days are snuffed out.
The grave is lurking in wait. And I
am surrounded by mockers.

God has blocked my way.
I can go no further.
He hides my path in the darkness.
I must pass away and vanish.
My hope is chopped down. God chops it off like
the trunk of a tree.

Job rebels against God. He rebels against his fate and curses the day he was born. He is a man afflicted with suffering, with true suffering. This way of suffering is not like some superhighway to God. It is, rather, a long, toilsome, thorny path. But there is one thing we believe about it. It is a path made holy by the sufferings of Jesus Christ, who also went this way. It is a path that leads to Good Friday, but then goes on to Easter Morning.

Good Friday and Easter Morning

At least one time, and sooner or later, our life's journey leads us to the way of the cross which Jesus followed. When we pass this way, we are refined like gold by fire. Life is not all fun and games. In the last analysis, there is always sacrifice and submission. There is always the cross that we must take upon us. Whoever denies the seriousness of life by wasting away his days will find things harder and not easier. *A worthless life is always more difficult for a person to bear than a life that is hard but full of meaning.*

One way or the other, life leads us finally to the way of the cross. Jesus Christ says to us, "Look at me. This is your life, too. Take it up, with all its burdens; come and follow me. But you can be sure that Golgotha is not the end of the way. The way of the cross does not end on the cross, but in resurrection, a greater life, that true fulfillment."

So we come at last to understanding what the word *God* really means. In the most ancient languages, this word meant "the One Who is called upon." And so when we ask ourselves, "What is God?" we have the answer. He is the One we call out to, the One to whom we cry, "Help us, O Lord."

4. Truth and Faith

A child takes life just as it is, unquestioningly. Everything seems obvious to him. He lives much like a little puppy. He has no problems and only little disappointments. He eats and drinks, scampers around and hides away, sticks his nose into just about everything, gets into fights. That's life. But gradually the light begins to dawn. He begins to wake up, to bestir himself. And suddenly he discovers something, quite amazed: "I'm alive! I exist! What for?" He discovers something else —the reality all about him—and wonders, "Is this what there is? Why is it here? Why is it this way and not some other? Why is there something and not nothing? Why is there as much as there is?" And now he begins to realize that this reality around him is not so obvious after all, but mysterious, strange, a riddle.

The Summons of Reality

Our spirit suddenly awakens and recognizes that this reality in which we are alive is the one great thing, the one thing that is truly meaningful. We know, in this moment, that we must live this reality with real passion and not just let it slip by without caring. We know too, that our lives are bound up with this reality. We know that we are called by it, summoned to know it and to harmonize our lives with it.

What is truth? Truth is this harmonizing of ourselves with reality. It is our responding to reality. It is a correspondence of our lives with reality itself. We know reality demands this of us. Reality is the one thing to which we have to bend. We must find out how to harmonize with it, find our place within it, and even —in the last analysis—obey it. We know we are called to live in accordance with reality. That is, we know we are called to do what is true, that is, to do what corresponds with reality. Every person knows that he cannot simply live however he wants to. You and I can't do just anything at all. *We must do what is true.* We must do what harmonizes with reality. *We must do what is real if we are really to live.*

Truth is knowing reality and acting in accordance with it. Truth that is merely knowing is not yet truth. Truth must also be *done.* Only when we both know reality and also strive to act in accordance with it do our lives become true. For many, this realization comes with earth-shattering force. It is an inner explosion. It's as if they are seized by this knowledge of reality. It is a deeply felt demand that drives them. They feel as if reality were demanding truth of them, were demanding that they know the truth, speak the truth, do the truth, and so live that they are fully in the truth. Whether other people think as they do or think differently carries no weight with them. They know that truth is not a matter of opinion. They know that truth is the most important thing that a person can ever have.

This truth, this demand put on us by reality, is a heavy charge. A person knows he is called and yet doesn't know where. He knows he is obligated to understand and to act, but feels weak and unequal to the task. This search for truth is a demanding, an exhausting way, a steep and difficult way up the side of a mountain. And this way becomes especially uncomfortable when a person has to act in accordance with truth even though this course cuts right across his own desires and the preferences of those around him. It is hard when he must refuse to go along with others, especially when they do not understand or disagree.

It is hard when he must say what others do not want to hear. It is hard to go it alone, hard to be an offense and scandal to others. Truth is uncomfortable. It is a burden, a heavy charge. It is the bearing of the cross.

For this reason, many refuse this burden. They know what truth involves, have a presentiment of its difficulties. They shudder under its impact and shake before its mystery. They don't want to see this great thing, this reality, anymore. So they bury their heads in their work, lose themselves in busywork, fill up their free time with gossip, and let themselves be carried away by TV reports of this new sensation or that new scandal. In this way they hide from the truth. The truth is no news event, no gossip, no local sensation. The truth is always the same, always difficult, always demanding, always discomforting. It is a great and profound thing. So many people look away from it. They cannot bear its light. They must go another, more comfortable way, a way that requires less effort. But even as they go this less tiresome way, some small sense of the truth remains with them. A little glimmer from that light which they have seen still shines on within their hearts. They carry some secret knowledge of that great reality, a sense of the profound things they had begun to discern. This little glimmer remains even within the person who refuses to see the light. It remains as a kind of uneasiness that reality still presents its absolute demand on human life. And if this little spark of truth didn't remain, then we would not be human beings anymore, but something less.

Still, there are some who never grow up, but go on forever like innocent children. Apparently they've never even had a suspicion of reality. They are busy with life, good-humored, innocent, naive. The mystery of reality is something these people apparently have never sensed, not even for a moment. It may be that there are many people like this who are always like children. God loves little children. Do these people remain like little children all their lives? Do they know anything of an absolute demand? Of reality? God alone knows the answer to these questions. He alone knows when he stirs a person, when he calls him to awaken to reality. He alone can make a judgment.

Who Calls Us?

We know that we are called, within ourselves, to truth. We know that the reality in which we live and which lives within us has put an inner demand upon us. But who can put such an inner demand on me? Who can put within me such a radical demand? Who can make me feel an obligation that touches the very root of my being? We may not ask this question of ourselves until much time has passed. We may be concerned about truth, struggle to meet its demands. We may really struggle to do justice to reality. In our struggle for truth and reality, we experience one thing: that no human being could put such a demand on me. Human beings can threaten me and can make life difficult for me. *But I know that I have an obligation to truth even when all human beings are against me.* So the absolute demand truth puts upon me doesn't come from human beings. Truth comes before every word that proceeds from the mouth of man.

Who can put this demand on me at the depths of my heart—if it's not human beings? Who requires from me an inner attitude of truthfulness that no human being could ever see? No dead reality could put this demand; not past history nor my own past could put such a claim upon me. Sooner or later I will die, but the demand of truth will still remain. This truth is demanding a response from me; it is calling me to responsibility.

Whoever struggles with truth comes finally to a day when he reverently acknowledges the One who is able to speak within him. He bows down before the One who puts an inner demand on him even when he is trying to escape. There comes a day, at last, when a person says, "I believe in you." In that moment the One who makes the inner demand and who appears in all the reality that surrounds us is spoken *to* by us. We say *You.*

Many search earnestly. But it is a long, long way. Many have a difficult climb up the high mountain of truth. Disadvantages of birth and family, the hindrances of neighborhood and environment all can make the journey more difficult. For some people, the way to the summit is much longer than for others. In the middle of their journey, though, the Lord God goes out towards them. They sought him even though they had not found him. They didn't know his name, but they still sought *him.* And he has found them.

Whoever searches for the truth is on his way towards God. Whoever wants to find and serve the great reality is journeying towards the Lord. *The search for truth is the search for God.* When man, in this search, finally finds God is something God alone decides.

Reality is the truly Holy One. Whoever cares about reality is religious, is reverent in the real sense of the word. He is a man of truth and he encounters God.

5. Science and Faith

Even a child asks questions. Asking why is a human characteristic. There's no way to stop this questioning without destroying man himself. Our questioning is a little bit like the curiosity one finds in animals. They stick their noses into just everything. They are curious. They have to learn about their world and gain some mastery over it in order to distinguish friends from enemies, to find food, and to defend their lives. Our asking why may, in the first instance, be like this curiosity in animals.

The Silent World

There comes a moment when many persons begin to start asking questions in a new and sharper way. These questions seem to arise out of an inner demand, out of some deep energy of life. And the persons who ask them have suddenly discovered the breadth and depth of reality: the heavens above, their own existence, the mystery of the world, and their own here-and-nowness in situations that are complex beyond description. So they begin to question: "Why is that so? Why does this world exist? Why am I here? Why is there anything at all? And why—of all the things that could be—are things this way and not some other?"

It's as if man made himself the judge of reality, subpoenaed it before his court, and demanded information and answers. "Why have you," the judge inquires, "put us into this world? With what right have you forced us to be alive?" Man asks why because he really wants to know where he comes from and where he is going. He wants an explanation of his own existence, his life, the universe in which he lives. He wants a clarification of the human situation in such an apparently strange world. And certain questions become insistent and cannot be avoided: "Why should I live the way I do rather than some other way?" "What power of disposability and control do I have over my life and the life of others?" With these questions, human beings search to understand their place in this world. If they don't find answers, then the world remains unclear and unclarified. When there is no clarification, then people become arbitrary. They begin to create their own goals rather that recognizing the purposes that already exist inherently within life itself. They make themselves the measure of all things. They see themselves as the most important thing in the universe; they think that man is God.

But the world we experience around us gives us no answer to our question why. It is silent. It is unexplainable. It is mute. We can, of course, explain this particular thing or that. We can, for example, explain why the sun rises in the east and goes down in the west. We can explain why some days are long and others are short. We can explain why there are genetic defects and why wars break out. But all human science finally ends in a dead end. Science discovers certain basic rules, but it doesn't help us to explain or understand anything more than we experience. All our understanding, explanations, and clarifications of the world come to an end at some point. That's the last stop. The process goes no further. There we are, then, still in the desert. We can go back to where we began and gather up some new experiences that we can also try to explain. But these lead to the same place—back into the desert. Science always leaves us off when we come to the questions: "Why is there being rather than nothing?" Or, "Why do we have this world and not some other?" The world never answers these questions for us.

Man can't come to terms with this unexplainable and incomprehensible world. He can't go on living in darkness. How shall he go on if he sees no meaning, no way, no ultimate purpose? He feels some demand upon him that comes from the world, from the great reality which surrounds him and in which he is rooted. Yet he feels that this demand is far greater than the particular things he experiences and which come and go. He knows that he is called to understand the reality of the world and his own existence and to live in accordance with it. He knows he is called to be "true" and to "act truly." If, however, he rests satisfied with the incomprehensibility of things, then there is no way that he could live his life in accordance with them. There is no way he could be truthful.

The World of Values

Science studies things that can be experimented with and proven. It has limited itself to this set of problems. That is its strength. What cannot be proved remains, from the scientific point of view, something unexplainable and incomprehensible. But is what is provable all that there is? Does science deal with the totality of reality? the totality of life? If it does, then isn't it the case that life itself—and the very presence of reality—would be unexplainable? Wouldn't that be the consequence?

But, don't we, in fact, discover something in the world that is more than what we can experiment with and prove? Don't we discover something more than the objects we can grasp clearly? What's the origin of this "more"? Human beings encounter all about them certain things that speak to their inner heart and must be regarded with respect. They experience the meaningfulness and worthwhileness of things. They know, from these experiences, that they are responsible and have obligations. They know reality has a value that should be taken seriously. They know that there is joy, love, peace, mystery, beauty, wisdom, and that which is worthy of respect.

What is this "more" that we discover in the world, but which yet is not ever really explained by scientific experiments and proofs. Experimental science can never discover what it is that, deep down inside, drives us and holds us to our obligations. What is it that causes us to feel reverent? What is it that makes us sense something is really important—so important, in fact, that we feel dutybound to care for it. (That's what duty really means.) What is the beauty that causes us to be overwhelmed by astonishment? What is it that lends to reality an importance that touches us within, and which we feel to be the meaning and value of things?

This reality that is more than the things that can be examined and proved by science can be called *value.* What is a value? What is valuable and worthwhile? The practical orientation of modern thinking usually understands *value* to mean *something that functions well,* technically or socially. Valuable, from this point of view, means *functional.* Hence as soon as a human being has no function in society, he is regarded as practically useless and valueless. His life is no longer regarded as worthwhile. But is this true?

The identification of value with function shrinks the idea of value too much. To have value means more than merely being functional. What it means can only be described: A value is something that is important to me, that I regard with unconditional seriousness, that touches and moves me in the depths of my being, that I acknowledge to be true, and that I recognize as meaningful. Value is something that I know without being able to prove it scientifically and by experiments. Value is something I am conscious of within, the source of my own inner conscience. Value has to do with love. In our experience of value, we encounter something so mysterious and so infinitely deep that no attempt to explain it could ever plumb its depths. We don't prove that things are values. We recognize and accept them as such. There is no way to demonstrate that value is value. I can only see that values are there and acknowledge their existence. If someone else doesn't see and acknowledge them, then I can't prove to him that they are there. All that can be done is simply to point them out.

Values are reality at its most intense. For reality is something that is active and effectual. Reality makes real. It *realizes* things. So values are reality, for what has this power to actuate and to make real more than values? Values are able to set people in motion, to motivate them from within, to make them want to live, to set them on fire. Values are what our love and hope and fears are all about. Values, in this sense, are the reality of human life where it most counts.

Values have a spiritual character because they can affect us in the depth of our hearts. They press themselves upon our innermost conscience and we know we are responsible. At the same time, we know their demand also comes from Someone Other. We know, in such moments, that we are in relation to this Other and also that we should respond—and be responsible—to him. We know we are being addressed by the Someone. The reality of all values is like some Other over against me. Because this reality addresses me, I feel responsible. I know who I am in this encounter with an Other who is speaking to me and calls me to be responsible. I know this One is a spiritual being like myself.

The Seal of the Spirit

We have seen that the world science describes is not the ultimate one. The fact of that world, its reason for being and being as it is, is something science cannot understand or explain. This world of ordinary experience is, in one sense, incomprehensible: its voids, its moments of desolation, its absurdity, and the sheer madness of its suffering. This world science studies appears to us often like a thicket, a darkness that cannot be penetrated, an impassable mass without any way out. The incomprehensibility of the world, in its depths, is evidence that the world does not contain its own explanation. The world science studies cannot tell us why it exists or exists as it does. The reason why it exists and exists just so are not within it. This world hasn't laid its own foundations and hasn't given itself its own form. It is passive.

What, then, is the basis of this world? What is the power that has caused it to exist and to exist as it does? We have already seen that the world about us is permeated and governed by values, by *Spirit.* For this reason, it appears to us to be meaningful, valuable, spiritual. We know we are responsible and have obligations toward it. Something spiritual encounters us in this world; an Other is speaking to us and calling our name.

So we believe we are justified in saying that this spiritual reality gives form to and governs the world we see about us. The Spirit establishes the world. This spiritual power is active and the passive world receives its mark. The world is like a wax that is shaped by the seal of the Spirit. What is this seal? What are the marks of the Spirit in the world? Values. Order. Love. Meaning. Truth. Life. Depth. Responsiveness. Duty. Conscience.

The Spirit is One who is there before us, One who calls us, One to whom we are responsible and to whom we respond. The Spirit is a personal being, One we call You. This Spirit has established the foundations of the world and even now still shapes it and gives it form. This Spirit is the Creator of the world, the Lord God of all creation.

The Religious Dimension

The great philosopher Wittgenstein once described things as follows: we can only talk about facts that are value-free in an ordinary way by using regular sentences; but we can't talk about true values, we can only point to them. This means, thought Wittgenstein, that our ordinary ways of speaking are not adequate to do justice to the highest things of life. No fact which is described by a simple indicative sentence can claim any inner obedience from me or elicit my aesthetic approval. Only those things about which we cannot speak possess the truest value. The really important questions—God, freedom, value, immortality—transcend the limits of speech and seem to abide in a realm art. Porter. Molencott

it cannot enter. For Wittgenstein one thing is clear: what is truly important and what is scientifically demonstrable are not at all the same thing. Everything that belongs to the higher realm of life, everything that possesses true value, lies outside the realm of scientific language. It lies beyond the range of direct speaking.

To summarize: Science is dependent on the experienced facts that can be spoken of descriptively. But descriptive language can only speak about value-free (value-less!) facts. Religion, however, is concerned with a higher realm which cannot be described by language—that is, cannot be spoken of as if some obvious facts were being described. Therefore, religious knowledge is concerned with a quite different level of reality than is scientific knowledge. The methods of systematic doubt and analytical criticism don't have the same results in religion that they have in science. In religion, we are concerned with a way of knowing that enables a person to experience values, a way of knowing that empowers a person to love.

6. Primal Faith

The heart of religion is in the experience we have of value. In our experience of value, absolute value, we meet the Absolute. From these experiences we first know the absolute, then specifically the absolute as God, and thus know God.

Hunger for Life

How do we experience these absolute values? Experiences of value occur when we desire something. But not every desire leads to this experience. We must desire something earnestly—really earnestly—so that we feel ourselves concerned and moved in the very depths of our being. We experience value only when we recognize something as meaningful, valuable, and fulfilling. In this experience of something as unconditionally meaningful we encounter the absolute, that is, we encounter what is ultimately valuable. Hence, it belongs to the essence of value experiences that we feel ourselves to be obligated, responsible, and called upon by life and what is good: We feel there is something saying "you should" to us, and sense ourselves to have failed and be guilty if we can't fulfill this "should." All true experiences of value have this characteristic: that we know them deep down inside ourselves as really our own and know that no one could ever take this knowledge away from us, or even have talked us into it in the first place. These values are experienced as deeper than reason, as unfathomable, as mysterious. We stand over against them in astonishment and reverence.

The basic value which we experience is life, is true reality. All particular values are merely aspects and embellishments of this basic value. For this reason, we are able to experience value everywhere and in all things. Whatever we do, whomever we meet, wherever we live, we experience value. The crowd about us, our friends, our spouses, our children, our jobs, our community activities, our trips into the mountains or down to the beach, the beauty of art and poetry and music, our housework and our family life together—all these can become value experiences and lead to a knowledge of value.

It would be wrong to think of these experiences in a highly dramatic way. Experiences of value happen as naturally, and without thinking, as do breathing and talking. They occur without our intending them, as spontaneously as life itself. If some country boy goes to the city because the life there seems livelier and more attractive, then it's life that fascinates and attracts him—life he consciously feels to be worthwhile. Or if some young people are hungry for knowledge and learning, then truth and reality are leading and drawing them—truth that they know is worthwhile. That's why such young people study and argue and search with such passion. Or if some young men and women search for love, then they believe that love has a kind of transcendent value. They believe that they have recognized something that is basic and central to life. Or when a teen-ager loves motorcycles or cars and wants to be an automechanic when he grows up, then what he really loves is life, a life that he recognizes as worthwhile.

Everything that has the power to move and attract us is life. Life means always becoming new and being renewed. For this reason, we love novelties, sensations, the change of fashions, the bright carryings-on within the city. We love the life that carries with it so many different values. Life also means the unfolding of our possibilities and the realizing of ourselves. Therefore, we love progress, the future, the making of plans for tomorrow. Life is also the desire for greater life. Life is strength, capacity for action, the power to do something. For this reason, a child reads cowboy stories and imagines that he discovers some special power to live and conquer the things in life. For this reason, a grown-up is fascinated by technology, for technology gives us some power to realize possibilities and to conquer the things in life. Life is the basic value we acknowledge, and it offers us the opportunity to become part of a greater whole. What life means is for us to participate in something more, far more.

Human beings are insatiable. They hunger for true life and real value. This is why they can never rest satisfied with what they have attained or achieved. They keep looking for ways to get beyond the limitations that bind them. They are restless wanderers towards new horizons from which they go on to still further horizons. They are always searching for something real, something that will fulfill their lives. Everything men and women do stems from this hunger for life. We hunger for totality, for ultimacy, for fullness of life, for the truly and completely worthwhile. Our knowledge of God arises out of our life experience. These experiences lead us sooner or later, consciously or unconsciously, to a knowledge of values and a knowledge of God.

The Hour of Decision

With the passage of time, we encounter unconditional value. Sometime and someplace this always happens.

And then we know: here is something important. If I didn't deal with this as important, I'd be irresponsible and life would be nonsense. My whole life is involved. The hour of decision has come. Now I have encountered the "you should" that speaks to me in the center of my heart. Now I know about the importance of life, about the unconditional meaning at stake that must either be chosen or rejected. I know it; I see it. Even though I see, I can still turn away. I can back out of this responsibility. I can refuse to hear even when I know I am being called. I can act like a child who pretends he doesn't hear his mother calling him home to lunch. He doesn't hear her call because he doesn't want to hear it.

We know, however, that we are moved. We know we have met him in the depths of our hearts. But we can act like children who are caught doing something they shouldn't: "Who? Me? . . ." We can hide ourselves from responsibilities—even by talking and thinking about them endlessly—until nothing is clear anymore. Unconditionally called? Unconditionally bound? To be regarded as absolutely important? "Let me alone to read my newspaper." "Don't bother me while I'm on the telephone." And so life goes on. But we've chosen even by our refusing to choose, by our preferring to remain blind to the choice before us. We have suppressed it. Finally, even our conscience no longer is alive. It doesn't feel or know a thing. It doesn't even know that it has said no to truth and meaning. Its no is shoved away in the bottom drawer of the soul, back in the darkness.

The basic decision a human being makes, however, remains whether he hears the cry of life and takes his value experiences seriously, or whether he refuses the call. Whether he believes he is unconditionally called, absolutely responsible, and bound to certain obligations—or whether he says no.

Sometimes the making of this decision takes years, even though we sense all that is at stake. We doubt, we question, we think over all the possibilities, we ask ourselves whether we are *absolutely* called, *really* asked to respond. Are things really meaningful? Is this thing truly that important? Is an obligation binding? No excuses allowed? Sometimes we struggle with these questions all our lives. But, eventually, we make decisions by our actions. By our actions we show whether we have heard with our ears and seen with our eyes and felt in the depths of our hearts—or whether we have decided otherwise.

But we make the decision one day. We really come to *believe* in values that are absolute. We believe in the values we have actually experienced. We believe that in the last analysis we are responsible, that something is unconditionally important, that there is an unchanging meaning to life, that we are called to live a certain way, and that what conscience tells us is real. Believing these things is the primal faith of humankind. No one can prove it to us. The decision is made, therefore, in the solitary depths of our being and at a time when we are alone. So it's our decision only, and no one thereafter can ever cut us off from it.

This primal faith includes, too, a readiness to acknowledge values that we otherwise might have ignored or overlooked. This is because the decision of primal faith is also a decision of primal love. Since it is basic, it makes us ready to care about values and to recognize obligations toward them. In this way, we obey the call of life. To care about values is nothing other than to love.

There is primal hope that now emerges, too. It

belongs to the very nature of our experience of life as meaningful. Our experiences lead us on toward the future. Wherever we act in accordance with meaning, the path of our life is moving onwards. Wherever we see that something is meaningful, our vision opens out before us. In this way, we have an intuition that our life journey leads us into infinity.

This primal hope is awakened, also, in a second way. Our experience of values brings us joy, strength, and fullness of life. This joy is nothing else than the fulfillment of life itself. Wherever we are doing what is worthwhile, we feel almost as if we had wings and were able to fly—even though the task we are about is difficult and causes us much pain.

An Inner Revelation

The knowledge of an absolute and unconditional value in life comes as an inner revelation in which the Ultimate Mystery allows itself to be known. The recognition of value is love. This love, however, flows from God, has its life from God, *and knows God.* A faith fed from the inner depths in this way is an encounter with God—even if there is no recognition that the Ultimate Mystery is named God.

"Whoever loves is alive in God and knows God." "Whoever does not love does not know God." "Whoever abides in love abides in God." Now we know why our Lord will ask, in the final judgment, "Have you fed the hungry? Have you consoled those who are sad? Have you visited those in despair?" He will ask about our primal faith, our primal love, and our primal hope. He will ask whether we have known the true values of life and whether we have responded to them.

7. The Decision of Faith

It's odd. The decisive facts of our life are experienced but not scientifically demonstrable. The existence of human freedom and responsibility, for example, is not a matter of science, but of personal experience. The existence of my own ego as something more than merely a collection of perceptions can be experienced, but not proved. My "ego," my "self," is no scientific datum. Nor is the human capacity to know truth. Perhaps, for example, our consciousness presents us with totally false images which have no basis in reality. No one has ever proved that a real world exists outside our consciousness. We believe that the contents of our consciousness are not arbitrary, but are received from a reality that lies beyond it. But we *believe* this. We cannot demonstrate or prove it. Science doesn't help us solve these questions.

In the same way, the inner relation that is established when we experience true values is also not scientifically provable. Science can't prove that, in such moments, we are linked with something absolute. Each one of us must make his own private decision for or against: do we accept this or do we reject it? Whoever has an experience of unconditional value or conscience *and also affirms it* is a believer. There is nothing more that can be done to prove or demonstrate the matter. Our primal faith and our primal love are at stake, belief in and caring about certain values which we know to be absolute and unconditional, important, meaningful, and demanding. These experiences also create our primal hope: that whenever there is something meaningful, the path of life leads into a future—even if we do not exactly know where it is.

Unavoidable Questions

The decision to make the first act of faith is not easy for us. To believe in an absolute relation, an unconditional "ought," and the reality of conscience is hard. Everyday this belief is threatened. A life lived in accordance with this primal faith is difficult and wearisome. And so the believer asks himself daily whether his first decision of faith is really irrevocable. Perhaps it was just a mood of the moment. Perhaps belief is only a wish. Perhaps it is only a fantasy that life has a deeper meaning. Perhaps we believe only because we can't bear to be alone in a vast cold universe, because we need to be protected by some greater being. Or, perhaps we affirm that reality is important because we ourselves want to be important. Perhaps we just can't bear the idea of being but pieces of dust in a vast universe going nowhere at all.

Do we believe that we are responsible because we want others to act responsibly towards us; and thus life will have a bit of order? Do we believe that there is value in the universe because we ourselves want to feel valuable? Are all the value experiences we have only our way of crying out, "I want to be worth something myself!"? Is our search for truth finally only our fear of being crushed under the world around us; so that we search to understand the world only in order to secure a place for our own lives? Is our desire for the absolute anything other than a desire to find a source of security? Isn't faith in reality an error, the mere surface of deeper inner desires? Isn't it self-betrayal? Betrayal of others? Aren't we, in the last analysis, alone—all all alone under the vast heavens? Isn't God only a projection of ourselves, a kind of mirror in which we can reflect on our own aspirations?

In addition to these questions, there are so many banal difficulties: our daily struggle with our own weariness and the pressures of life. Does it make any sense at all to try and believe these things when life is already hard enough? Isn't it easier to eat and drink and let heaven worry about the fall of the sparrows (if heaven wants to!). Why try to reach beyond what we can touch with our hands and see with our eyes? How can we follow the guiding star of faith throughout our lives? Isn't faith only a flash in the dark night to which we must finally surrender? Why should it be given to us to know more than what we can taste and grasp and see and hear? Don't we outdistance ourselves as human beings when we talk about a "primal faith"? Isn't the renunciation of such faith more honest than the painful attempt to fly, like Icarus, beyond our limits? Isn't it more respectful to keep our feet on the ground rather than to attempt the climbing of uncertain heights?

But after we have experienced the heart of religion, we can no longer put it or anything else blithely aside. We can't ignore life's religious dimension even if we know that it will always be impossible to explain scientifically and analyze precisely what it is we have experienced. We can only say, "I have encountered a Mystery." And we must then try to say what it means to have faith in that Mystery and to live out of that faith. Otherwise, we will not be able to maintain faith in the midst of the noise and rush of daily life.

Making Sense of Faith

Man must, therefore, try to interpret his radical religious experiences and investigate their basis. He must do this in order not to surrender these very experiences. His interpretations are merely attempts, attempts to get into focus the Mystery that has encountered him. Somehow he has to lay hold on it and comprehend it. But such comprehension is always dependent on the point of view and special clarity with which he has experienced the Mystery. His comprehension, therefore, has something to do with his intellect. It gives a greater emphasis to one or another aspect of the experience he has had.

Some people interpret the experience this way: "An incomprehensible Mystery has encountered me. I want to respond to this fact reverently. It is the very fulfillment of my life. But I can't say more than this." Those who speak like this actually describe God, but by the name of "Mystery" (even when they don't think that "Mystery" is an adequate name for God). Such people may then think of themselves as agnostics, because they think they can't say more than this. But they have already said enough. They have already acknowledged that they must respond *reverently.* They say this even though, as agnostics, they fail to give any reason why this is the most appropriate response. Which is why this interpretation of religious experience is insufficient: it doesn't really explain anything. Perhaps such people don't really dare to go further and give a thorough account of their belief—because that would carry even further consequences.

Others interpret their religious experiences like this: *"All* the reality that seems worthwhile and meaningful to me is truly God. I mean *all."* Such people consider themselves pantheists since they say, "Reality itself, in all its aspects, is God." This interpretation implies that a human being is the highest and most important thing in the world. In some sense, too, it implies that human beings are alone in the world. But what, then, puts the demand on us in our innermost conscience? Do stones? And are we responsible to the milky way? Of course not. It isn't stones or clouds or spiral nebula that put this demand on our innermost conscience. Rather, it's something other than our experience of these things. We feel ourselves addressed by some Other, by Someone whom we speak to as a person—"You."

A third group of people explain their religious experiences as follows: "Man reaches towards something that is more than just food and drink. He wants to go beyond his own situation and transcend himself." This particular interpretation also says something about the experience. But does it say that in it we encounter some Other? Does it say we feel ourselves called to responsibility by this Other? Isn't it a bit misleading to suggest that man is like a small David who tomorrow will have gone beyond himself and become a Goliath, and the day after will have gone still further and become practically a god?

A fourth group simply describe themselves as atheists. "Such experiences don't have anything to do with God, but rather pertain to our relations to other people. Others put demands on us and we are responsible to them alone." Such people think of themselves as "humanists" because they feel responsible only to mankind. There is no denying that this interpretation draws attention to an important aspect of religious experience. But is it really true that it is only other people who speak to us in our innermost conscience? Don't we feel ourselves called by all of reality to a knowledge of the truth? Isn't there a higher demand upon us that makes us search for meaning, even cry out for it? Can humanism explain the awful suffering of mankind? Can it explain the fact that we exist? What about those in a concentration camp, burned alive in ovens, or those being shipped off to die by freezing? Or the red-hot slivers shoved under the fingernails of a torture victim? What about the excruciating pain of that moment just before a person's senses become numb?

"You"

We have experienced an Other who calls us. This seems to be meaningful, worthwhile, and valid to us. We have dared to name this Other—even though it exceeds all words. Dare I name this Mystery "You"? The Buddhists don't because, precisely because, this Mystery is so much more than words can express. Even the Old Testament says, "You should make no images of God." All that can be said is that this word *You* falls far short. And yet I must say it: "You—the one before whom I feel myself responsible. You—the one who is my last refuge. You—the Ultimate Reality, my fulfillment, the meaning and love and power of my life. *You.*

This kind of unconditional meaning, value, and love is everywhere. This spiritual reality, which we have dared to address as "You," is present in all things, shaping and moving them. All the things we experience around us are formed by Spirit, by You. This world which cannot be explained through itself has been created and is sustained by the one we call "You."

All the ways we attempt to portray this Mystery are false and inadequate because the Mystery can't be fully conceived. We are like little dwarfs. We can't encompass the Mystery with our minds. We are grateful for whatever smaller and usable conceptions of God we can manage. We're not big enough to manage more. And we thank you, Oh Lord, that you allow yourself to be contained in such little and inadequate ideas of you which fall so far short of who you really are. We thank you for your humility, for your willingness to appear to us dressed in such unsuitable and unfitting ideas as we can manage. We are never irritated by anyone who lacks a fitting idea of you; we are never upset when someone clothes you with the best *he* can manage—even though it falls far short of what would be truly suitable—for we are only little people and have no better way to think of you.

But one thing we do know, O Lord. We know that even though *you* is but a human word, we still dare to call you "You." We dare to say this because we love you and because you speak to us and because we can be together with you. All people have called you Father. They wanted to say that you are the Ultimate, Absolute, Meaning, and Love that gives life and form to all the world. You are the One who gives me my life, too, and shapes it by your will. All people know that they are formed by you. Therefore, they call you their Father, their Creator, You.

8. Proof and Faith

We know that science deals with the world that can be experimented with and tested. It is concerned with everything that belongs to nature: the study of society and politics; of psychological behavior, techniques, and organization; of physical, biological, and chemical laws. But science can't tell us about things beyond nature because it deals only with demonstrable things. Science is honest whenever it deals with what can be tested. But human beings know about something through their value experiences that lies beyond the reach of science. The basic experiences of religion cannot be the object of scientific investigation because in the last analysis they involve personal knowledge and require personal recognition and decision.

"Metaphysics"

But human beings have to clarify this "more-than-natural" dimension of life. They need some explanation, and a foundation for their religious experiences. Otherwise, they could not maintain such experiences or develop their long-run implications. This "more-than-natural" dimension is called *meta-physics. Metaphysics* means "more than nature" (for *physics* is the Greek word for nature). "Metaphysics" suggests a "more than." Because this "more than" is not scientifically provable (at least in the sense of the natural sciences), its explanation cannot be undertaken by the experimental sciences or by purely rational means. The explanation of this "more than" is, first of all, a question of human perceptiveness and sensitivity. It is an ability to perceive and experience this "more than." Not all people possess such perceptiveness in the same measure. Some have more and some have less (including, of course, many spiritual people).

Secondly, a knowledge of this "more than" also involves rational understanding and intellectual ability. Many people are deeply sensitive to this dimension and yet can't put what they experience into words; they can't explain it either to themselves or to others.

Hence, it's not surprising that there are so many different explanations of this "more than," this thing we call "metaphysics." There are as many as there are people, cultures, and even individual human beings.

Human beings attain to the foundation and root of all religion by a knowledge of values, an ultimate and supreme knowledge of values, a knowledge of what is absolute. But the development of human life in the past several centuries has not cultivated a sensitivity to values, but, rather, has stressed increased intellectual analysis: rational, technical, scientific, logical knowledge. During this same period, metaphysics has also become colder and more *purely* intellectual; it has been less and less understood as a rational explanation of an incomprehensible mystery that has been experienced. In the hands of thinkers who are interested only in purely intellectual activity, the preoccupation of metaphysics has become simply "proving or disproving God's existence." The real roots of religion —the knowledge of values, their relations, and their life-giving function—have simply been bypassed.

So, the task of metaphysics—defined now as a purely rational activity—has changed and made "progress." But not only metaphysics. Religion, too, has enjoyed dressing itself up in intellectual clothes: slogans, programs, and new catechisms. But in all this, the basics of religion get covered up and snuffed out —like glowing embers underneath the ashes.

Orthopraxis

Down with Metaphysics?

And so it came, as it had to. Since the cold, logical, analytical capacities of the mind were no longer able to know the living God (that is, *prove* his existence—so the saying went), human beings began to look for new ways. A choir of voices began to cry out, "Down with metaphysics!" This choir of voices angrily pointed out that metaphysics was not scientific knowledge in the usual sense of the word. It pointed out that metaphysics came to various and contradictory conclusions. It asserted that metaphysics was useless, mythical thinking, an archaic remnant of the past which was no longer relevant to scientific thinkers or modern men. The protest concluded that metaphysics had no further use since its results could not be established with scientific certainty and subjected to experimental verification.

Therefore, some voices urged, let us be done with metaphysics and get back to the really basic things: the knowledge of values and their realization through human action. The worthwhile life, they urged, consists in "doing what is right." Rather than metaphysics, let us have *orthopraxy*—doing right. That should be enough, for all else is uncertain and unprovable.

This orthopraxy wants to tell us: Be heroic! Be conscientious! Be good! Accept your responsibilities for others! But, the question remains, "Why?" And to ask this question is right, for we have minds and we don't want to do what appears unreasonable. Unless there are reasons, we don't do anything. This orthopraxy—which tells us that sheer morality, doing right, is enough—actually forbids us to think and ask questions. But the question "Why?" still is being asked, the question about the meaning of the world that is "more than" science knows about. This question "Why?" is the metaphysical question. It is the question about the meaning and foundation of moral striving itself. It is the question about the basis of our doing right.

To interpret and understand our deepest human experiences will always be important for those of us who ask questions. But metaphysics must be conscious that it is *interpretation* and not *scientific explanation.* And we must become aware once again that knowledge of values and their relations is not something we can derive from science. Values can't be ascertained by computers or mathematics, nor can they be understood and established by pure reason alone. Knowledge of values arises out of the encounter of man with the absolute, and not out of some encounter between computers and God. In every experience of value we encounter a mystery of love—and computers can't love.

Experiencing God

The word *proof* is used today almost exclusively in the scientific sense, in cases where demonstrable matters are at stake. But we have seen that the knowledge of God is not something that is established by science. God is no fact to be demonstrated and tested. God can only be known in absolute experiences of value. He can only be known in situations where love is at stake, for God is love. Therefore, God can only be experienced by a kind of loving. God is not known in some objective way, as in reading the temperature from a thermometer. There is no knowledge of God that is "disinterested." Only one who is first *interested* is able to know God. Only where something important is at stake, something really worthwhile, does God appear to man. But the very characteristic of science is to know things in a disinterested way, in a way that is uninfluenced by hate or love. From a scientific point of view, it makes no difference whether the investigator is fascinated or bored. Hence, one thing is clear: science, pure cold science, can never establish the existence or nature of God.

We are uneasy when we use the word *proof* in talking about knowledge of God today. The word has been taken over by science and it's better, therefore, that we let it go. If we are looking for a knowledge of God comparable to the proofs we get from science, then no such knowledge can be attained. But there are still ways to know God. For example, we can describe how people arrive at a knowledge of God. We can do this. But we can't give people some "information" about God—as if we were to say, "Here, read this book. You'll learn all about it." There is no such information about God; knowing God isn't like knowing the multiplication tables. If I want to make another person understand why I believe in God, I can only give an account out of my own experience. I can do this because the basis and root of religion are only understood through experiences of value—and in the end a person must have these same experiences.

So, I can try to elicit or awaken value experiences in others. I can try to uncover certain questions that people have buried down inside themselves. I can encourage others to let their own inner desire to know the foundation of certain experiences come to the surface. I can explain to others why I interpret my own experiences as I do. I can tell how long I struggled where "evangelism" and dramaturgy converge.

until I finally became certain that I was addressed by God within—and I can explain why I believe such an absolute demand can only come from the Absolute. In all these ways, I can make other people understand the experiences *I* have had. Other people may be helped to understand or interpret or clarify their *own* experiences from what I have said. But none of this involves *information* about God. It is, rather, more like the understanding that takes place in friendship or in love. Whenever someone finds happiness, or joy, or peace, or the meaning of his own life he also wants his friends and brothers and sisters to discover this, too.

then what about a "theologized society"? one that 'talks'

Knowing God

What has been said so far must not be taken as meaning that the knowledge of God is merely a feeling. Experiences of value must be founded on sure human knowledge. This means that I come to know God not only through my feelings, but I also *establish* my value experiences and my intuitive sense of God by intellectual reflection. Both in the First and the Second Vatican Councils, the bishops affirmed that "God, who is the origin and end of all things, can surely be known through the natural light of human reason as it reflects on the created world." This affirmation is derived from the teaching of the Bible, which says, "Whatever can be known about God has been revealed to men. God Himself has revealed it to them. Since the creation of the world, his invisible being can be perceived by the eyes of the spirit in all his works, his eternal power can be perceived—and also his divinity." When Scripture says "can be perceived with the eyes of the spirit," it means more than merely understood with the intellect alone. The "spiritual" person is the person with a warm heart, a person who is open to a greater reality, a person who knows about values and can love. Such a person has life and spirit; hence he is able to perceive God.

Lord, we are grateful to you that you let yourself be seen, though not comprehended. You let yourself be seen in an incomprehensible way.

The importance of the journal, that they help us remain open to the greater reality. Who knows about values can love.

9. The Crisis of Faith

We should be honest about the situation. Today there is a serious crisis of faith. Everywhere in the world today there is discussion about the most fundamental of all questions: the existence of God. Many people in Africa and Asia—as well as in Europe and America—are simply atheists. The decision about God is more intensively debated and more in doubt than at any time in human history. And each of us is asked what we think about this question. Each of us contributes to the ultimate decision one way or another, either by speaking or remaining silent, or by opting to avoid it altogether.

The Historical Background

The volcanolike bursting forth of this crisis came at the time of the Enlightenment, 200 years ago. At that time, Western man rediscovered the power of his own thinking. The motto was then formulated: "Have the courage to live by your own ideas." Everyone wanted to *rethink* all the things that had ever been thought before. No one wanted to accept anything merely because someone before him had affirmed it. So there was a thoroughgoing rejection of all the authoritative things that had, till that time, determined human thinking: tradition, revelation, the Bible, the Church, and ordinary customs. For the modern man, the principle of judgment became his own personal insights.

Therefore human beings became critical. Everything was investigated and dissected. The method of systematic doubt was employed in order to determine exactly what could be retained of the old and what had to be swept away. This principle of systematic doubt became the methodological principle of the sciences and, in fact, of thought itself. The activity of doubting became, in fact, the general method and condition of human life. "Critical reason" now began to go to work. The examinable world was examined and man did not find God there. The consequence was that man decided God's existence could not be proven by the methods of science, by experiments, or under laboratory conditions. Man decided that God could not be known in a value-free way, that is, by an investigation uninfluenced by either inclination or disinclination. But does a bridegroom choose his bride in this scientific way? Or a girl her lover simply by the method of critical reason? Of course not. And the same is true of finding God. *The Critique of Pure Reason* (Kant's great work) put an end to all efforts to establish a purely intellectual basis for God's existence. But it also generated an aversion to metaphysics—since metaphysics is not understood or controlled by the methods of experimental science or pure intellect. And at this point, man began to ask: "Well, then, where are you, God?"

Among the most important modern thinkers was Auguste Comte, the French sociologist. He contended against everything that was not provable by scientific experiment or which transcended ordinary experience. He rejected, thereby, all metaphysical thinking and all the proofs for God. Everything of the sort seemed a complicated fantasy to him. Comte gave importance only to what could be proved positively: hence, *positivism.* After Comte, the German thinker Ludwig Feuerbach threw the match in the powder keg. He described religion as a secret wish that human beings projected into the universe. "Whatever man wishes to become," said Feuerbach, "he imagines his

Gods to be." One can see why, with such arguments, people began to suspect that all religion is merely an illusion, a projection into the universe of wishes and feelings that exist only in man himself. Religion, on this view, is a mirroring of what man is in himself; it originates in man's sense of "the divine" within himself that he then wishes to find in reality outside himself. It is, in short, only a projection. Then Sigmund Freud carried the argument further: our ideas of God, he said, are not only projections—but are projections of infantile mother or father images. In this way, the argument then forces the religious man to question his own innermost motives: "Why do *you* believe?"

The answer to this question cannot be given by any scientific experiment nor by any election or questionnaire. The answer can only be given by individual persons in their innermost depths where they encounter and seriously examine their own motivations and feelings. Every person must decide the matter for himself. It's a simple, either–or affair. "Is there something or someone who is more than I? Or am I the highest and most important reality I know?" There's no other alternative. Each one of us must face this decision within: either . . . or; either You . . . or I. There's no third choice. No other possibility than these two. Therefore, I come to believe in God because I know that I am unconditionally called to decide and know that I can't just decide arbitrarily whatsoever I prefer.

Karl Marx opposed religion because he thought that people used it to maintain systems of authority that were actually unjust. "Do we have kings," he asked, "by the grace of God?" Modern sociology has surely exposed the relationship between the religious ideas of a society and the structures of authority within it. Of course the ideas of God that people have derive to some extent from their social and psychological experiences. Karl Marx rejected God because he thought he could only reject the religiously justified systems of authority in this way. He rejected the idea of a transcendent "beyond" which, he thought, offered false consolation to humankind. A consoling belief in a realm "beyond," thought Marx, actually cheats people out of life in the here and now. It does so because they then neglect to change the conditions of their life in order to become happy. On this view, religion is like a sweet dream that prevents people from taking hold of their real world and improving it. This is why Marx described religion as an "opium for the people."

Of course, Marx is right as far as he goes. All religion can be used in this way, that is, *misused.* All religion can be misunderstood. But what can't be misused? And what is safe from being misunderstood? Is modern Marxism, for example, invulnerable to having its original ideas misunderstood? Are Marxist ideals protected against all misappropriation and misuse? Where is there any world—or anything in the world—that is spared ignorance, misunderstanding, injustice, and misuse? That a thing can be misused is no argument against its proper use. If it were, then we should not use anything at all, ever.

Temptations of Our Time

But the crisis of faith today has still other, even banal, causes. Often it has nothing to do with great "problems," but with simple human failings. Many people have "never had it so good before." In the West, we have become relatively rich and are protected against the worst kinds of need and suffering. We have everything; we don't need anything—not even God! The temptations of a "fat generation" probably weigh a good deal more in the balance than a hundred truly serious questions and problems about "God's existence." Satiated people don't hunger for anything more—and we know it!

We weren't always as clever as we are today. Two thirds of all the researchers and scientists who have *ever lived* are alive and working today. We think we're learning a lot and can get along without other teachers. Especially teachers about God! To feel this way is one of the temptations of an "educated" and "well-read" generation. This generation wants to be autonomous, and is so, more than in the past. The very collapse of authority is a symptom of this. People today don't want to be owned and shaped by anyone else. Not even by God. Not even by God? That is another temptation of an age that wants to rule itself.

No young people were ever so free from taboos and inhibitions as the young people today. Is it a generation without laws? And without a ruler? Another temptation of a pleasure-oriented society! Man has never before been so powerful as in our time. Our technology lets us reach for the stars. What will prevent us from becoming all-powerful? The Almighty God does not impress us any more. Another temptation!

These temptations are human, all too human. To try to account for them by some theory is not necessary. This is how people act. One can understand. But the issue still remains, and it is serious. The issue is: faith in God? Or not?

The Loss of Religious Experience

But the heart of the crisis lies deeper still. The root of religion is religious experience. What happens when this kind of experience fades away? Doubt about everything that can't be studied by scientific experiments has become widespread. Only such experiments count. But who can make experiments with God?

Never before has mankind been so rushed and ragged, so far from a contemplative, prayerful, conscious relation with God. The individual is wedged into the heaving mass and carried along by it. Millions of people wear the same clothes, have the same TV, follow the same fads. Life is programmed for us; we live automatically. Does the individual even need his own conscience and conviction anymore? And yet can anyone find God unless he has a conscience of his own, feels an individual sense of responsibility, and reflects on his own life? If we don't recognize and care about values anymore, then there can be no more knowledge of God. If we don't recognize values, the basic root of religion is buried; if we don't care about values, human faith, hope, and love become cold and die. The freezing up of love is closely related to godlessness. The Bible describes it this way: "Many people will lose their faith. . . . Because godlessness prevails everywhere, the love of most people will grow cold."

Are we surprised, then, that when people today ask about God, they get no answer? Are we amazed that many have even stopped asking? Do we even wonder that this crisis shakes the entire world? A world that no longer recognizes God is not able to love any more. And what will happen to a world in which love has grown cold? A world in which all values become rotten and left behind? Why should we be surprised when meaninglessness is promoted and advertised everywhere—like some new gospel! Why even pause when nothing counts for anything anymore? When no one regards anything as important! Why wonder that there is no joy or peace? That obligation is regarded as a laughable old-time thing? That responsibility is rejected and a sense of guilt regarded with shame?

Nietzsche had a prophetic sense of what would happen when faith in God was submerged in darkness, when knowledge of God came to an end and God no longer lived in the human heart:

> You will never again pray, never again worship, never again repose in boundless trust.
>
> You do not permit yourself to come to a standstill before an ultimate Wisdom, an ultimate Goodness, an ultimate Power. You do not permit yourself to unharness your thinking. For your seven lonelinesses, you have no permanent Guardian and Friend. You live without having a view of snow-capped, sun-filled mountains. You no longer have an Avenger, an ultimate, authoritative Corrector. There is no longer any rationale for what happens—no longer any love in what will befall you. Your heart, though it must only find and need no longer seek, no longer has a resting place. You are opposed to any kind of ultimate peace.
>
> Oh man of renunciation! Will you renounce everything? Who will give you the strength to

do that? No one has ever yet had this strength.

The End of Man

Where there is no more God, there is also no more man. That is the moment when man destroys man. Once man's fascination with God has disappeared, then man is debased and made vulgar. At that moment, he becomes the man who uses mankind as mere experimental material and as instrument of his purposes. This is the man of the concentration camps. This is the man under an all-powerful state.

The crisis of faith is a crisis about *man*. How can man endure? The fundamental import of this decision should be recognized by us today. There will be a separation of those who believe from those who do not believe. There will be a division of those who hope in God and those who hopefully hurry from disappointment to disappointment. There will be the disjunction of those who love from those who merely calculate. There will be those who want to be human and those who have forgotten that that is what they are.

10. The Hour of Faith

Unless I'm deceived, the world is now experiencing a moment when God is addressing it with a new demand. The world's capacities and power are rapidly expanding. Along with this expansion, there must also be an increase of love, hope and faith. Otherwise, the discrepancy between the gigantically expanding brute power of man and the powerlessness of his love will be too great for the world to bear. If our love, hope, and faith are not strong enough to direct and lead our newly unleashed power to some good use, then this power will destroy human life. The sorcerer's apprentice will no longer be able to control the sorcerer's might.

The Demand of the Present Moment

The scientific discoveries and inventions of our time lead to an immense increase in man's powers. Atomic physics has gained control over matter. Space programs lead man beyond the confines of this planet. Genetic technologies give man power over biological nature. We have unlocked the code of life, deciphered the language of the living cell, and prepared ourselves to take control of the future evolution of man. Computers are now beginning a new industrial revolution whose future effects are simply immeasurable. The power of humankind has expanded beyond measure. For every person in this world—adult and child—there already exists enough fissionable nuclear material to equal eighteen tons of conventional dynamite. Every single person in the world today could ignite eighteen tons of dynamite! Who is going to harness all this power? It is dangerous when the muscles grow and not the mind. And it is dangerous today when the technical capacities of man have so increased, but not his power to love. We are like big children running around thoughtlessly with loaded guns and pointing them at one another.

This is a critical moment in world history, a moment when God is asking us whether we really intend to deal honestly with him. It is an hour when God is bringing the world to an awareness of how far short its love and faith really fall. It is an hour when God's demand is falling upon us, an hour in which we have to make a decision. One path leads to a mankind without God, to a human freedom which does not know itself to be dependent on anything—not even on love, faith, and values. The other path leads to a realization of all the things that are worthwhile in life, to a recognition of the reality of conscience, obligation, and responsibility. To an acknowledgement of God. This is an hour when all mankind must decide.

God meets us wherever we encounter something that is unconditionally meaningful and right. He meets us wherever we experience things that are worthwhile and important, wherever we sense responsibility or feel ourselves addressed by life. Religion encompasses the whole of life. Religion is an encounter with the whole of reality. Wherever we encounter values in this world, we must recognize these values and do something about them. Wherever we encounter values—anywhere at all in the world—we must believe and we must love. However, no one of us is easily inclined to engage ourselves with all values and all of life in such an encompassing way.

Therefore, the religion of most people is a narrow and egotistical affair. What most people see in religion is their *own* meaning, their *own* security, their *own* consolation, their *own* life power. For such people, it's too much to recognize the reality of God in *all the world* and to feel responsibility everywhere and towards everyone. So they reduce God to someone they meet in their privacy and aloneness, to one who hears their petitions and good-night prayers. They go to church like people paying their tribute and taxes, hoping that God will take care of them, too. They hold fast to some religious rituals and ceremonies—and in this way try to tell everyone that they have a relationship with God. But they've completely forgotten or lost the meaning of the rituals and ceremonies. They now are just external husks from which the inner spiritual meaning has totally oozed away.

Yet Jesus Christ told his contemporaries, "You pay your tithes on the mint and dill and cummin, but neglect the most important things of the law: justice and mercy and faith. These are the things a person should do—and he doesn't have to neglect the other things to do them. . . . You catch a mosquito who fell into your teacup, but you don't even notice you're swallowing a camel whole. . . . You wash the outside of your cups and bowls, but leave the inside full of greed and self-indulgence. . . . You are like gravestones painted white: you look beautiful on the outside, but underneath you are full of dead bones and rottenness. So you appear to be outwardly righteous in front of people, but inwardly you are full of deception and foulness."

The Waiting World

The narrowing of the scope of external religion to the confines of the liturgy has taken place all over the world. Where are the people for whom this is not true? Technology has expanded, but love has not increased alongside it. Political power has grown into something gigantic, but faith in values and the love of all the worthwhile things in life has remained small and dwarfed. The world feels that this is the case. Yet the world wants a religion that has the power to heal and help it. People expect religion to prove its power *in the world.* They want to see that it is effective *here and now.* If religion can help and heal the world, then people will know it is true. The loss of respect for religion is so great precisely because religion seems to be irrelevant when it comes to coping with the difficulties of life and useless for dealing with the problems of the here and now. Religion has become ensnared in the shell of private life. It has become salt that has lost its savor. It lacks the power to inspire the world.

The world reproaches religion today, saying that it is not paying attention to the actual crying out of life, that it is not entering into the real sufferings. For this reason, religion appears deaf to God's command. The world reproaches religion for not paying attention to the sins and failures that really count, for not helping where there is real misery, for not responding at those points where God is really demanding obedience. The world says that religion no longer understands God's own language, that it is no longer able to understand the values of life as the language God uses to speak to us. The world says religion is disobedient to God because it doesn't obey God *when and where* God wants to be obeyed. Religion today does not understand that to love all the values of life is to understand them as God's way of speaking to us.

For this reason, so many people today reject God

and religion. Religion seems to be useless and irrelevant to the world and to the true values of life. The world rejects God and religion *in the name of true humanity and true values.* This is why the present moment is a special crisis of faith for us. God is demanding a more encompassing religious attitude, a breaking out of the narrowness of cult and externals. God is demanding a love that reaches forth more widely. He demands lives that are truly ready to care and sacrifice themselves for what is beautiful and true. Otherwise, we will experience the bitter consequences of the fact that our technological-political power has grown beyond our ability to make it serve human ends.

Where God Dwells

We must learn again that we meet God not only in prayer and not only in some afterlife. We must learn that God can be met wherever we encounter something unconditionally important and know that something ultimate is at stake: in the meaningful, the worthwhile, and the serious things of life. Every time we encounter the values of life and know that some demand is being placed upon us, God is coming to us. Wherever we know we are called to cherish certain values, there God is, too. This is what the Bible means when it says, "He who abides in love, abides in God." Wherever people love, they meet God. But of all the places where we love, the most important is the place where we love our fellowman. That's why the Bible says, "Whatsoever you have done to the least of my brothers, you have done that very thing to me."

We must learn again how the reality of God meets

us in the whole of reality. We must learn again that God is already present to us in this world, that he speaks to us through it, and that he is with us when and wherever we respond to his command to love.

It is a dangerous limitation of God when he is thought to exist only in a transcendent "beyond." It is a dangerous limitation of God when people think that this is a secular "world without God." A world without God can only be a godless world. If people no longer understand how to find God in this world, then this godless world will be an unmerciful one.

There is only one reality, and not two separate "kingdoms." God is not separated from the world in one kingdom or the world separate from God in its own autonomous sphere. There is no place in the world where God is not present. He is here encountering us wherever there is love or obligation. He is here to meet us whenever there are values or meaning to be found. Here is where God "dwells."

This does not mean, of course, that the world of ordinary experience is the only dimension of reality. There is still the world of values and truth and higher meaning that cannot be reached by science. All our value experiences point beyond themselves to this higher realm of values. There is a reality that lies beyond the power of death. In this sense, there is a "beyond." We believe in this life beyond all death because we know that the love of God is stronger than death and because we know to whom we are responsible in this life. But life beyond death does not mean that God is found only after death and that he is not present in the midst of our life in the here and now. God is always in our midst.

11. Faith in the World

If God meets us in the midst of the world and all its values, then the great liturgy of our lives takes place in the world itself. This "secular worship" or "worldly service of God" is the real test of faithful human beings. A secular religiousness is required of us today. A religion that is narrow and narrowly conceived is not able to do justice to the demands of the present age.

The New Religious Ideal

The great service that is required of us today is to hear God's demand that we obey him—and then to obey him! It is to pay attention to God's call to obedience in the midst of the needs and sufferings of the world wherever we encounter them: in our families, our work, our children—and wherever there is war, hunger, poverty, loneliness, despair, bitterness, abandonment, guilt, doubting, and yearning for a meaning to life.

Our faith consists in the fact that we hear this call of God to us and understand it. Our hope consists in recognizing these goals and working for them. Our love consists in our cherishing these values and these persons and in our giving ourselves over to them. This is true worship; this is the service of one's brother; this is the way to love God.

Above all, we must hold up this worldly service of God as the great ideal for the younger generation. We must hold it up as something which responds to the challenge of the present hour. Who offers ideals to youth today? Get more money; have more fun; put more power in the motor! But where are the ideals that can really be held up to young people today?

Must not a world whose ideals are money, fun, and power in the motor finally suffocate and collapse simply because it lacks any true values? Young people must be shown once again that it is worthwhile to give oneself to those things that are truly important. They must be encouraged to hold fast to the great things of life, to the things that really inspire them, to what is worthwhile. And this finally involves God, true joy and peace, the existence of this world, the fulfillment of their own lives, society, and the state.

The same thing must be said to those persons who hold great responsibility for society: to civil servants, politicians, teachers, and those who shape society and are its leaders. "You are people on whom thousands and millions of others depend," we must say. "You are the ones who can lead humanity *either* into egotistical self-concern and vulgar consumerism *or* into the loving service of others, social responsibility, and deeper fulfillment of life. If you yourselves no longer live responsibly, how can you expect responsibility from others? If you yourselves have no sense of conscience, how can you expect others to fulfill their duties and be conscientious? If you yourselves no longer take work seriously, how can you think that others will consider their work as something important and worth doing? What do you really expect of people? Of business? Of art? Of education?"

The same thing must be said to all business executives and managers. "If you don't feel responsible for the people who work under you, why should any worker feel responsible for what he does? If you only do what is right because some union is threatening to strike, why would you expect any worker to do what is right? If you produce meaningless and unnecessary

Values

products merely to make business profits, why would you expect any meaningful work from your workers? Or, to sum it up, if you yourselves no longer recognize values, then how can you expect all your activity to be other than worthless?"

If the word "capitalism" only means "making money for myself," then this means the final destruction of the world. But if it once again meant "responsible use of money, values, and the possibilities of this world," then the world could live again. If it meant *this,* then there would be responsibility and happiness and a sense of what things are important, and we could breathe deeply once again.

God's Striving within Us

But the new, divine service that is demanded today is even more encompassing and broader in scope than is apparent so far. This service exists not only in our response to the command of God that we have experienced in this world. It is even more than this. We ourselves are a part of the world. If God is present in the world, then how much more is he present in *us?* God is the living presence in every human being. Our life is soaked in the reality of God. All of our life power and human potential is—like the world—colored and vibrant with God's power. Our inner drive and yearning is often itself unaware just what it desires and strives for. But, at heart this yearning we have for meaning, purpose, truth, a true place to live out our lives, a creative unfolding of our potentialities—all this is God's desire and striving within us. This inarticulate yearning is thirsting for those values that God wants it to find. This mysterious desire comes from God himself.

Often this longing and striving takes a secular form that apparently has nothing whatsoever to do with human love or love for God. For example, a person may feel an inner striving to find a vocation in which he can better realize his potentialities. A person may struggle for scientific knowledge. A person may yearn for a bit of renewal, a moment of peace, a small place to be at home. Wherever there is real striving after values, God is present in our desire. Our doing and aspiring, our attention and our obedience, our personal sacrifices are all ways of serving God if they grow out of love and lead to love. They are all a worldly service of God that intends to make something real of the good things in life.

Of course, there is a striving within us that is not the striving of love. There is also dark and unholy desire. That's why the worldly service of God does not occur in every form of human striving, but only where there is true love and the aspiration towards real values. It does not take place where mere egotism holds sway. We know that real values are intended when we are inwardly obligated, responsible to something more, and held fast by our conscience. We know real values are at stake if we feel ourselves called and take the issue seriously for its own intrinsic worth. When real values are at stake, things will be difficult and be a burden. But real love continues even when the way is hard, and it persists even though it is criticized. Real love reveals itself where people act in accordance with their conscience. And true service of God (true worship) takes place where, even in dark days, people believe in values, believe in mankind, believe in truth, believe in God. The courage to sacrifice oneself, to risk one's own life—that is the mark of the great service that God wants from mankind today.

The New Saints

A worthwhile life, a life that cherishes values, is also a fulfilled and therefore a joyous life. *Joy is nothing other than fulfilled life.* It is a life filled with power. Wherever we see meaning and know we are called to live for it, there is hope and power that stems from God. Reverence is there, too. Reverence is everywhere we recognize things to be important and cherish values—for there we also cherish God. This is true not only for individuals, but for the whole society. This is the only way that a society can have peace and the inner strength to control those powers let loose in our time. And, too, this is the only way a society can be happy, no matter how high its standard of living may be.

Wherever people desire lives that are worthwhile, there will also be an increase of freedom. The person who has lost his values is worthless and has become a slave. A person whose life is worthless looks constantly for something worthwhile. But he looks for this in money, or cars, or new clothes, or sex, or security, or pleasure, or just plain novelty. If he looks here, he never will find love—for love can be found only where there is something of value.

People who look for the meaning of life in things and not values are forever restless and searching for something. They are the slaves of "gimmee, gimmee." There is a compulsive "must" that enslaves them. Love alone can make them free. It is the only way. Without it there is never freedom, but only anarchy. Love frees because it gives us confidence. Love lets the other person have his own freedom—because it trusts and has confidence in him; and love takes freedom for itself, because it has confidence both in itself and others. Where love is, there is even an increased freedom of human beings in relation to God. All the little constricting fears that might have held us—fear of hell and suffering and death—they are now done with. Where there is love, a person knows that he is not imprisoned by God and that God does not impair his freedom. Love is never little; love is never constricting. Love is what makes us free.

In this hour the world needs a new hallowing and it needs new saints: saints who will show us the great true worship of God, and who will lead us in the new worldly worship. For them, God has become all in all. They have received eyes that are wide open and are able to see the values of this world. And they can love all living things everywhere within it. They believe, in the most literal and realistic way, that word of Scripture that says, "And God saw all things and saw that they were good."

The new saints of the world know themselves to be called to be near to God in the midst of the world. They know that they are bound to God here and now. They know how to tell the difference between the worthwhile and the worthless. They know about struggle, sacrifice, and love. And they are clear that God lives *in this world* and that in this world they are close to him. These are the priests of the great new worshipful service the Lord of the world awaits from us today.

12. The Mystery of Faith

All the great ancient religions of the world knew about the relationship between a knowledge of values and the times of quiet. They knew that there was some connection between awareness, meditation, mysticism, prayer, contemplation, and a recognition of what was worthwhile. The true depths of life are not seen if one just casts a quick tourist glance in their direction. They are seen only if one strives to see deeply—by reflection, by developed awareness, and by learning to be quiet. But all these things are missing today. People are mobile, caught up in a fickle, restless go-go-go. People have become conditioned to be one-sidedly intellectual and rationalistic. Who teaches them anything about knowing values? Who shows them the way to live a worthwhile life? Who even talks about these things anymore?

A Thousand Names and the One Great Secret

The old religions all knew how people attained to an experience of values, love, and the absolute. For example, one described it as "going down" or "letting oneself sink down into the Tao." (The *Tao* is a name for the Ground of all Being.) When you go down deeply and arrive at the ground of all things, there you will discover the Tao, the absolute and unconditioned —God himself. For everything in life is rooted in God, and so when you trace the roots of all things back to their ground, you find God.

Other religions describe this as a process of heightening awareness, increased inwardness, and spiritualization. They want, in this way, to say that when a person seeks to get to the heart of his life, then he comes to God. That is, when a person seeks to become aware of his own thoughts, aspirations, longings, aggression—and to understand the world around him and the meaning of his own life—he actually uncovers a fountain of Living Water, God himself. For everything in life is rooted in God. We ourselves, including all our thoughts and feelings, are rooted in God. A person who seeks to come to himself in these ways also finds God. Deep down, at our very roots, where we find God, there is a little soul-spark that is burning. And as we draw near to it, it begins to illuminate our inward being.

Other religions describe this place where we meet God as the place of "Nonaction" or "Doing Nothing" (which Laotse called the "Wu-wei"). What they wanted to express was that we must become still if we wish to know God. God cannot be found in the midst of frantic activity and hectic life. He can only be found when we have readied ourselves for him to visit us.

Still other religions speak of "reflection." They want to say that when people carefully observe the life around them, when they pay attention to reality, then they will see more than they can see with their eyes. This "seeing" is more than just a looking at things. It is a seeing into the depths of life, recognizing the values and the meaning, and penetrating the absolute good.

There are some people who talk about "mysticism." They want to describe, in this way, how the person who has been reflective and quiet encounters the Mysterious, the Incomprehensible, the Secret that transcends our grasp. One of the deepest and most profound thinkers of our age once said, "The most elevating and yet profound feeling that we, as human beings, can have is an experience of the mystical."

Who said this? Albert Einstein.

This is the intense, glowing heart of all the great ancient religions of the world: the experience of the Mysterious, the Unutterable, the Unconditioned, the Absolute, the Hidden, the Incomprehensible. But it is precisely this hidden, incomprehensible Mystery that all these religions acknowledge to be the truly real, the reality active in all things. The encounter with this reality is the source of all religions—and has been so for centuries. The everyday religious experiences of people are traces of the bright, full experience of the Mystery. Even when someone sees the coming dawn, before the bright sun has yet appeared, there is light enough to illuminate his life and give him a sense of the meaning, end, and value of all things.

People have called this Mystery by a thousand different names. But they always knew that none of these names could adequately describe the Mystery. None of these names could really plumb the Great Secret. Even when we use the word "God," we know that this word only illuminates the Mystery in the smallest way. If someone is deaf and can't hear music, then musical notations cannot give him any sense of how music actually sounds. In the same way, if someone has no sense of the Mystery, the Unconditioned, the Utterly Valuable, the Ultimate Reality, then all the books about religion that have ever been written will not help him in the very least.

A Crisis of Prayer

The crisis of faith that we experience today derives essentially from our loss of quietness and a sense of the mystical. We could call this crisis of faith a "crisis of prayer," though prayer is so often misunderstood today as asking God for this or that—or else it is conceived as mere formal repetition. The sickness of modern man is his senseless chasing around, the pace of life that simply wears him down. People today are harried by their work, by their world. They are driven and worn out by all the possibilities available to them. They are seduced by profit and oppressed by the merciless machinery of the work process. Only those who can keep up with the pack can avoid being trampled underfoot. If one begins to slow up, he is stamped down.

Life has become a drunken brawl. We are drunk with work, drunk with possibilities, drunk with expectations, drunk with advertisements; we are drunk with noise and more noise and still more noise. Colorful signs and loud slogans assault us on all sides.

We are simply worn out. But when someone is tired, then it's easy for him to close his eyes and begin to drop off. That's our situation today. We are tired from the pace, from the chase, from the noise, from the very goals and demands that we make on ourselves. We are exhausted, emptied. We may have enough energy left to go to a movie, read a paper, or have a glass of beer. But we don't have the energy to reflect on the ultimate and deepest things of life. Thoughts about such deep things require energy. And most people don't have enough energy for such reflection anymore. The eyes of the spirit are closing up, and we are losing our sight of God. The ultimate and deepest things of life, its innermost meaning, are being lost to us.

At the same time, we become strangers to ourselves. We no longer can recollect ourselves. We no longer have the time to come to ourselves, to gather ourselves inwardly. We live on the most superficial level, held spellbound by mere things, captive to all the bright ads and sales. We are harried and hunted and driven. We aren't even responsible for what we do anymore. There is no longer any "I" behind what we do. We have lost ourselves; we have become like machines. We feel some things, but we are no longer alive. The events that happen in the world seem to occur independent of our wills. A "law of things" begins to operate and take over. We are ruled by things rather than ruling them; for we have fallen asleep or become powerless. Each one of us loses his "I." Things just happen to us; we do not choose them. All mankind today is held spellbound by things, fascinated by the "law of things." And so people are ground down and destroyed by things. And this will continue to happen until people are able to find their way back to their true selves, to the "I" within.

Faith in God is wavering today because people no longer have time or strength for quietness and a personal relation with God. We've solved the problem of going to the moon. We will soon be able to direct the evolution of the earth. We are in control of the power of the atom. But we do not seem to be able to solve the problem of time. We do not seem to be able to have time for God. Nor have we strength for him. Why can't we solve these problems?

God will become ever more strange to us. We don't understand anymore what strength one gains from a relation with him. We don't understand the strength or freedom that come from loving him. And so God becomes something a bit weird. Modern man no longer knows the God who is Love. For this reason, he is afraid of his own freedom and independence. He no longer knows that love both frees others and makes oneself free. Not knowing this, many today flee from God and from *awareness.* In this way, the gap between man and God gets wider and the abyss before us grows deeper.

Time Out

Perhaps one might clarify the consequences of this thoughtless chase that dominates our generation. Here is a simple example. God is love, and so the encounter with God is a bit like the encounter that takes place in marriage. Time must be set aside for love, otherwise love will die. If a married couple will set aside time for each other, then they can talk with and find each other; they can overcome things that separate them; they can get closer and be near. In this way, their love increases and their relationship become closer. And they become one. But if both people no longer have time for their relationship then what can one expect? They become increasingly strange to one another. And the same thing holds true for God. For God is love. But where there is no time for love, then the relationship becomes estranged and cold.

The seed of religion is rooted in experiences of value. Wherever we know ourselves to be responsible, obligated, and bound by our conscience, there we meet God too. So if we want to encounter God, we must take time for reflection. Then we will be able to figure out what is meaningful and what is meaningless. We must ask ourselves what in our lives makes sense and what is nonsense. If we take time for reflection, then we will become clearheaded and sober. We won't be merely existing, but will be questioning, reflective, and aware persons. In the course of time, such reflection leads to conviction and considered belief. Whoever has such conviction also has character.

We have to take time for meditation. What am I actually doing? What do I really want? We need the courage to confront our own lives. Can I be responsible for what I am doing? Can I really recognize my obligations? Can I discriminate among them? Know which are mine? Know what I should be doing? We need the courage to struggle until we're clear about what we should and what we shouldn't do. In this way, our conscience gradually grows stronger. Our inner lives get clarified and purified. Only if we take our own lives and actions seriously and try to give an account of our actions and failures to act will we encounter God and attain a degree of wisdom.

All things are rooted in God, including our own lives. The deeper we penetrate our own lives (learning even our secret wishes, fears, aggressions, and hopes), the nearer we come to God. The more we can account for in our lives—the more we know our obligations and responsibilities—the nearer we come to God. For he is the ground of our lives. To find oneself is to find God: that is an old saying.

But if people lose their power to meditate, deprived of a sense of life's meaning and living in a superficial way, then the darkness begins to spread. Our ability to see into the depths of life weakens. Our capacity to sense the larger meaning disappears. Until the only thing we can see is our own ego. Then all the drives and powers within us are torn away from their true goal and anchoring in what is essential. They become independent and separated, prey to whoever wants to capture and use them for his own purposes. This is how a person becomes dangerous both to himself and to others. A person who lacks a sense of meaning becomes confused and muddled. How can mankind make important decisions if it has lost its sense of meaning and has become confused and mixed up in this way?

Whoever really seeks to get to the ground of things and his own life will one day find far more than merely value and conscience. For one day the fountain of life itself will begin to flow, and that person will know that *God is there.* This is an inner revelation, some really true encounter. It is a mystery so great that it can't be approached more closely than this. But it will give a person power, confidence, and a true homeland. Now, for the first time, a person knows who and what God is—and what the Word of God really means to say. Yet the God who is experienced always remains a mystery, an incomprehensible reality, and an uncontrollable power. But this is the encounter which, as Einstein said, is the most elevating and most profound that we in our lives can ever have. Now a person senses the immeasurable greatness of God. And now he begins to understand for the first time that heretofore strange language of religion: Light. Illumination. Infinity. The Absolute. New Life. Conversion. Sacrifice. Eternity. Meaning. Truth.

Not God Alone

There is nothing that cannot be misused. There is nothing that cannot become an occasion of temptation. Even religious experience can become such a temptation. Even the experience of "God alone." A person can now begin to search only for the repetition and deepening of this mystical perception in prayer, quietness, and adoration. Exactly this same kind of thing can happen when a person has found someone to love, someone who means a great deal. When someone falls in love this way, he can hold fast to this experience of love so that he neglects his work, his obligations, and gives up the larger society and its life —all because he has found that special person.

Today we know that this is not an acceptable way to love God. The time in which we live presents us with an important and serious task: to find God in the universality of reality, to discover him in all his works, and to respond to him by an all-encompassing sacrifice. Today, we must love not God alone, but God in all things. This is what Scripture teaches: that God is all in all. We must find in all things and situations a way to love and to love God. This is the faith which can prove itself in our world. This is the faith that can be known to be true, precisely because it proves itself. This is the encounter with God which is obedient to the real call of God.

We find the God who is real where we obey the real call of life to us. When we stop up our ears because we don't want to hear this call, then we no longer encounter the real God. Then religion becomes the very thing that people so criticize today: believers who are deaf, religious persons who are blind to their true obligations. And when we do not obey the call of life to us, we also become persons who evade the demands of truth, concocting images which we set in the place of the God who is real.

Today God demands that the faithful of this world hear his call as a universal and encompassing command to pay attention to his presence in all things. We must break out of our narrow, self-imposed religion. Only the religious conscience, sense of responsibility, and unconditional conviction can succeed in controlling and directing the powers and energies that have been unleashed in our times.

13. The Fullness of Faith

All the great saints and those who have had experience testify that God is an incomprehensible mystery. He is the inconceivable, the ungraspable, the unspeakable One for whom no name is appropriate. He is the Unfathomable, Groundless, Nameless One who, in the last analysis, remains unknown. In the same mood, the Old Testament tells us, "You shall make no images of the Lord your God." Every image of God is only a dead God made of wood—and not the true Living God who exceeds every conceivable reality. In the same way, the New Testament says that "God dwells in unapproachable light." And the Church, in one of its councils, taught that "everything that we can say about God is more untrue to him than it is really like him." Nevertheless, we can and must search for a knowledge of God because we simply must try to find the origin and end of our lives. We must do this because we cannot begin to understand ourselves unless we can understand at least something about this inconceivable God.

"Having" God?

Perhaps this can all be made clearer by using our familiar example. Knowing God is like knowing another person whom we love. We first get acquainted and then learn to love them. We come to the stage where we are ready to share our lives with this person and to risk living together with him for a lifetime. We know this other person better than anyone else in the world knows him. We know his innermost thoughts and feelings—and yet . . . this person whom we know so well and whom we may have loved for a lifetime will remain a mystery to us. This person will always be someone new, even someone shockingly different. This person will always be presenting us with the totally unexpected. One could never imagine for a minute actually "having" this other person, for love never binds or "has" people. Rather, love is always a new, free gift that comes through the other person—and tomorrow morning the form of this love can be completely different.

It's the same way with God. You may think you know him as well as you know yourself. But he remains a mystery. We "have" our God in the sense that we have given ourselves over to him and want to live out our lives in relation to him. And yet we don't *have* him. Love never pins anyone down. God is always close by, forever surprising us, often making us joyous, but sometimes filling us with dismay. And we always are knowing him anew. Which means that we haven't really known him. He is greater and quite different from anything we had known before.

The Meaning of Grace

Faith in God is similar to love between two persons in another respect. Whoever really *believes in someone* needs some kind of response from him, some kind of confirming word. The other must reveal himself to him. For example, we might love someone whom we believe we know very well. In such a case, we trust this person, put our hopes in him, and love him very much. Yet something essential to full belief, full trust, and full love is still missing. Only when the other person reaches out towards us and confirms the trust that we have put in him does our commitment mature and attain fulfillment. Only when our affection is accepted by the other person, and confirmed by his expressing his own feelings, is my love for him finally crowned. And only when my belief in the other person has found an echo and confirmation in him has my belief become a bridge that joins the two of us together.

Two people are like two shores separated from one another. Neither one can build a bridge over to the other shore all by himself. Only when *both* try to build a bridge can the two be joined. Only when each puts up something from his own side can the two be joined in the middle in a firm arc that bridges the gap between them.

It's much like this with our trust in God, even the God we have longed for, sought, and known. We have had certain experiences; we long for him; we believe in and we love him. And yet the response from the other shore can still be missing. We can start to build a bridge from our side to his. But if he doesn't also build a bridge towards us, reveal himself and reach out toward us, then our faith remains a mere extension of ourselves, a bridge that has been begun, but which remains incomplete. If God himself does not reach out to us, then our trust in him remains trembling and fearful. It still remains filled with our own longing. If God himself does not speak his word to us when we cry out to him, then our love for him lacks its fulfillment. Only if he speaks and answers or, more exactly, only if our cry is an answer to his original call, only then have we found one another. Only then is the bridge put up. Only then can we go across.

Where God does not reveal himself and reach out to us, our faith in him remains always in doubt. We may have religious experiences, experiences of unconditional value, experiences of the absolute. But even these experiences of God are experiences of love and, therefore, experiences of something *given,* something that is *sheer grace.* We experience our being bound to God as suspension over an abyss: held up by God, carried by God—and yet still hanging and swaying over an abyss. Our feet don't reach down and touch a firm bottom. All of our experiences—the experience of unconditional meaning, the experience of valid and worthwhile love—these are all real, profound, and fundamental experiences of life. However, they are not in themselves the kind of independent foundation from which one could construct an edifice of logical consequences. All of the love we experience, and the things it includes, is grace. It is a gift. But we cannot grasp and hold fast to this love in the same way that we can possess some object. We can't take it and look at it and test it, even if we have decided, under its impact to live in accordance with our true conscience. We can't grab hold of it and measure its reality even if we regard it as completely true and valid. This love remains always a gift; it doesn't come from me. It is as if someone holds *me* up even as I sway over a deep abyss.

We might want to reflect on our religious experiences. More exactly, we almost feel that we must reflect on them, think them over, and try to uncover their fundamental meaning. We need to come to thoughtful conclusions. But all this thinking is only a building that is constructed on top of our experiences of grace. The foundation of this building (that is, the experiences of love we have had) actually hangs over a deep abyss. It is sustained by God, borne by grace. At least this is how all those who have honestly and passionately struggled with God have experienced the matter. They experience him as the one who bears them up and holds them in his hand.

As long as God has not replied to us as an Other, as long as he has not revealed himself and answered the cry of our faith towards him, our faith remains a shaking reed. Faith here is an expression of deep longing and the result of radical searching for God. Such faith can inwardly prepare a person to encounter God. In his search for truth, a person is made ready to gamble his life. He is ready to risk his existence to attain this good. This is the saint who searches for God with all his heart, and all his soul, and all his might. To such a person *God will come.* God will not deny him what he seeks, for "he who seeks shall find, and he who knocks on the door shall have it opened to him." However, man's question about God can never be settled from his side alone. Faith stretches out its two arms towards God, but finds nothing to grasp hold of to swing across to the other shore. For darkness is all about. Practical objections are heard on all sides. There are many points of view in the world today. So faith is tempted and made anxious on all sides by the many opinions, proposals, false ways, and detours. A person can try to create certainty for himself by believing he can lift himself up by his own bootstrings. But this is not faith, only self-deception. It is not faith, but mere self-glorification. It is the impatience that refuses to admit that it cannot carry itself across to God on the other side by its own strength.

A true and full faith is not the result of metaphysical speculation that builds up a point of view from certain prior experiences. *God has revealed himself.* Without God's revelation of himself, faith is at best a necessary longing, hope, searching, and striving for God. Without this revelation, faith is still readiness and openness to God. But it is not yet full faith.

Revelation Fills the Earth

God dwells in unapproachable light. No one can make a sculpture or picture of him. He is the incomprehensible, unthinkable mystery. We love him, we long for him. We seek the Absolute, which is the foundation, beginning, and end of our existence. But we are only able to comprehend him—this incomprehensible reality—when he himself comes forth from the darkness and meets us. We are only able to know him—this unknowable One—when he reveals himself and shows himself to us. And whoever has long questioned and long sought is one day grateful that there is an answer. He is grateful that Jesus Christ comes as the answer of God, the word spoken by God to us, the self-presentation and revelation of God himself. "Whoever sees me has seen the Father."

Only to the God who answers and reaches out can man entrust himself. Only in the God who reveals himself can man full confide. To him man gives over his entire existence. The bride entrusts herself to her bridegroom when her searching and questioning have found their echo and answer in him. Only then does trust become *entrusting,* does courage become *encouragement.* Only then does one seek another and give himself in a lasting bond that unites him with the other. Only when the questioner finds one who answers does love become that bridge which joins two persons to each other. Only then does love become a bond, a binding together, a covenant.

the prophetic

God has revealed himself to human beings at all times in history. Ancient man had no written alphabet and therefore described his world mainly in pictures and by myths. He experienced God in such pictures that portrayed life forces. Even in the Old Testament, these ways of revealing God are still found. In storms and in lightning they experienced the power and the reality of God. In the liberation of the small tribe of Israelites from slavery in Egypt, they experienced the "mighty hand of God." In the victory over their enemies, they experienced the helpful presence of God. In all the signs of life, God revealed himself as the Strength, the Presence, the Anger, the Revenge, the Righteousness, the Good, the Forgiveness. God's name in the Old Testament is "Jahweh," which means "I will be there." God was everywhere in the midst of these people, everywhere in the midst of Israel.

Later in the Old Testament, as the Israelites gradually lost their pictorial mode of thinking and experience, individual persons who were impressed by God and strove mightily towards him, became the bearers of revelation. They were the *prophets.* These prophets proclaimed the will and presence of God. People believed in the God who revealed himself in the prophets because they could experience his powerful presence in their lives. God revealed himself in the prophets, and the people believed. The prophets themselves experienced the demanding and loving power of God as sometimes an inner and sometimes an external revelation.

But finally the yearning and searching and crying out of mankind for God became overwhelming. Where is God? Why has he left us alone? As mankind evolved to the stage of written culture, these questions in their hearts became sharp and self-conscious. People wrote about them, reflected on them. Their urgent question was, "Where is God if we cannot see or perceive anything? Why should he be so far away? God cannot abandon us altogether." And now came the moment. Now at last people were ready to understand that *what they encountered was not a mere picture or work of God, but God himself.* They were no longer babes, but adults who knew what they were looking for and so were able to recognize it when they found it. Jesus Christ is the presence of the inconceivable, and utterly great God now abiding with us. If God wants to be forever with mankind, then must not God already be here in our midst? If God loves mankind, then can he hide himself from us? If God loves us, then can we cry out and he not hear our cry? If God loves us, will he not come to us?

We believe in Jesus Christ. And we believe that he will be with us until the end of the world. He will be with us in the Church which makes his word present, which makes his answer present, which makes him present.

14. Jesus Christ and Faith

It is hard for people today to see in Jesus of Nazareth the "eternal Son of God." However, it has also become increasingly clear that the very disciples and apostles who accompanied Jesus also found this hard to see. Only very slowly, hesitatingly, and gradually did they recognize the Lord in all his greatness and dignity. The Bible shows this to us, step by step. Even John the Baptist asked, "Are you the one who is to come or are we to wait to another?" In fact, *before the resurrection itself had taken place* not even one of the apostles knew and acknowledged the full dignity of the Lord. They were "blind," says the Bible. "Even when the loaves were multiplied, they did not attain insight. Their hearts were blinded," says Mark. So, it would be demanding too much to expect people today not to have to go through a similar development. We cannot expect that people today will immediately and fully understand the glory of the Lord: that he is fully God and man.

Man . . . and God?

The disciples of Christ recognized their Lord in his full brightness and glory only in his resurrection. What actually happened then? The most ancient texts of the New Testament speak of appearances of the resurrected and glorified Christ. The resurrected and glorified Christ let himself be seen by men. This was an immediate perception, but it wasn't as if they saw him just as we see, hear, and taste things in ordinary life. The word "appearance" means that this perception was given to them by God. The natural sensory organs were not adequate to perceive the resurrected and glorified Lord. Only the capacity that God gives human beings so that they may experience and believe in him was adequate. When Jesus Christ "appeared" to them, the disciples knew that he was alive and that his life continued. They knew that God revealed himself to them in the One who was resurrected. Now there was light on their path. They saw before them the Living One, the One from whom life cannot be taken, the One who is Life itself.

Neither the disciples nor the early church were clear at first what it meant to acknowledge Jesus as both God and man. But they felt his closeness to God. Christ said of himself that "the Father is always with me." And the disciples certainly felt this and believed his words. Hence, it wasn't so difficult for them to see the Son of God in Jesus Christ, since Jesus himself had spoken of God as his "Father." But this didn't mean that at that time they already knew Jesus to be a *Godlike Son.* This didn't mean that at that time they acknowledged him to be both man and . . . *God!* In the same way, we shouldn't be shocked if many people today come to understand Jesus Christ slowly and gradually. "In Christ, God is meeting them." They see in Christ a man who is close to God, a holy man in whom God acts and speaks. But they don't yet grasp the full measure of his greatness. Only after the resurrection were the disciples themselves fully able to know who Jesus is. He is the one the Old Testament calls "the Promised Messiah." But even in the developing thought of the early church, Jesus was not yet seen as the "God-man." He was, rather, recognized as one who had been raised up by God his father to sit at his right hand and have all power in heaven and on earth. But he was not yet understood to be the "God-man."

It took a long time before the young church conceived of Jesus in a full and fitting way—as one with the Father, as sharing his being: God from God and Light from Light. Only when this was understood could the church then say that the woman who bore him is the very "Mother of God." For this reason, we realize today that people need the time to grow slowly in their understanding of Christ. Today's questioning and critical person must slowly rise to a full knowledge of Christ. He must go through several stages of understanding, exactly as the disciples and the early church went through several stages. If, in preaching Jesus Christ, we try to skip over some of these stages, then Jesus remains incomprehensible. The whole richness and fullness of Christ can only be plumbed by someone who has lived through and reflected upon all the stages of understanding.

Whoever tries honestly to live with Christ is faithful, even if he is not able to grasp the full richness of Christ. On the other hand, there are some people who confess Jesus Christ to be *both God and man,* but have not worked through all the intermediate steps and affirmations. For them, Christ is not really an example, the Lord of their lives. For them, he is not really a teacher and prophet of God whom they hear and obey. Whoever does not live out his entire life *together with Christ* is lacking something in his faith—even if he confesses Jesus Christ as both God and man.

An Empty Grave?

We see Jesus not only in the golden raiment of his godhood, but also in the fullness of his human life. We certainly will say yes if people today see first of all the *man* of God, the *man* sent from God, the *man* who lives close to God. But we will never agree that anyone preaching the Christian gospel may deny the godhood of Christ and claim that Jesus is simply a man. The point needs to be raised because some have said that Jesus "was only a man—no more and nothing special; and that if he was more than a man in any respect, he was but a higher type of man." If Jesus were only a man like us, then he would have been just as much prey to every human error that we are. But Jesus is for us far more than a man. For us he is the Word of God, the Answer of God, the Presence of God, the Love of God, and the true Son of the Father.

As Christians, we understand that the knowledge of the resurrection which the Apostles had was a knowledge given to them by God. It was a knowledge that is more like faith than physical seeing. Today, many people suggest that the report of the New Testament about the empty grave of Jesus should not be taken literally. An appearance of the resurrected and glorified Jesus would have been possible even if the grave had not been empty. But we must not lightly abandon the clear statements of Scripture. It doesn't help to make the direct statements of Scripture into "symbolic modes of communication" unless there is some real necessity to do so or some really compelling new knowledge. Jesus himself knew how hard it is for human beings to believe in realities that are invisible. In the very time of Jesus, there were also persons who had doubts about the resurrection of the dead: the Sadducees. It is a great miracle, of course, that human life is able to continue beyond death's doorstep and to move into Eternal Life and Light. Human beings can believe in this victory of life only with the greatest hesitation. It is hard to believe in that life beyond death that God gives to us. This is the very reason why Jesus left a realistic sign of his resurrection for his disciples. This realistic sign showed them that what they had experienced was no empty dream, no deception worked by their longing hearts, no human error. Moreover, the Jews in the time of Jesus would never have been able to conceive of a resurrection that was not also a resurrection of the body. This was due to their general world view and way of thinking. For the Jews of the first century, therefore, the proclamation that the Lord had been raised from the dead wouldn't have lasted even a day if the grave of Jesus had not been really empty.

As Christians, we have to give an honest account of our faith in the resurrection of Jesus Christ. We live our whole lives in terms of this faith. Therefore, we need all the "signs and mighty deeds" that Jesus gave to people then and gives to us today. A miracle cannot, of course, make a person believe. There were many contemporaries of Jesus who saw his miracles and yet did not believe. A miracle is a call of God to us, an impulse to faith, a sign of the power, presence, and concern of God. A miracle can be recognized as a miracle only by faith. Only in the light of faith can a person know that *here* God is at work. Without such a sign from God, a person must ask himself whether he's not being taken in by some sleight of hand or flight of fancy. We need the signs that the Lord left to us so that we might know him. We need them if our faith is to be solidly grounded, reaching down to the very bottom of things. Whoever blithely pushes these signs from God aside and interprets the Bible as a "symbolic" or "mythological" way of speaking should not be surprised if his own faith soon goes awry. Precisely this reason is behind Pope Paul's recent warning that "the historical value of the inspired witnesses about the *fact* that Jesus was *bodily resurrected* is not to be denied or to be interpreted in a symbolic or mythological fashion."

A Mechanism of Cruelty?

Many people today also find it hard to believe in the redemption of mankind through the death of Christ. They claim that the idea of a sacrificial death of Christ is a "mechanism of cruelty." They cannot understand how God could require the sacrifice of a human life so that justice could be satisfied. To such people, we might say: redemption occurred by love that reached the outermost limits. What has redeemed mankind is not the pain, not the blood, not the destruction of Christ's life, but his love. What has redeemed us is that love because of which he sacrificed himself. The death of Christ is only an expression of this love that reaches the outermost limits. This love—existing in a world that is filled with envy, misunderstanding, egotism, and power—went the last step, went unhesitatingly into battle with the powers of this world.

Whoever loves in an unconditional way knows that this love also involves sacrifice. It evokes the opposition of others, angers them, and is persecuted by them. Anyone who really loves must ask himself whether he too is ready to make a sacrifice. As Christians, we know that the love of Jesus—the very love of God—has redeemed us. So we cannot accept as Christian any preaching that says, "Jesus neither proclaimed nor prophesied nor interpreted his death as having any redemptive meaning."

We must oppose, too, those who hold that, "It is very unlikely that Jesus wanted to save the world by dying." Whoever makes such a detour around the Bible does harm not only to faith, but, more significantly, to the very foundation of faith. If we are always tearing down the foundation on which we build, then we need not be surprised if the whole structure of faith one day collapses. For this reason, unless there are weighty reasons to the contrary, we must reject that interpretation which regards Jesus' prophesying his own suffering as a later addition to the gospel accounts.

"Everything Goes?"

There is one more thing that gives people difficulty today. They regard the commandments of Christ with considerable fear. They are afraid of the freedom Christ proclaims. They believe such commandments are unrealistic, utopian, and impossible for the world today. Such assessments of Christ's commandments put many people off from seriously engaging themselves with his teachings. To them, therefore, it must be said that all the commandments of Christ are concentrated in one specific duty: the love of God and of man. What this love means is keep one's eyes open and allow oneself to feel those demands that arise from the needs of others, the distresses of our age, and the fears and troubles of those around us. This is the kind of thing we must tell those who are already so hard-pressed so that they do not become discouraged and give up before they've even begun.

On the other side of the matter, it is unfortunate that there are those who think that the Church's proclamation of freedom means that anything at all is permitted: "Everything goes!" Such an interpretation of the gospel leads to the breaking of all the old tried and tested rules of human living together, even to the abandonment of the principles that sustain family life and children. The commandments are signposts of the love of God, and it is intolerable to tear them down as if they were mere archaic taboos. It is good that we are able to help people understand things better today in a freer atmosphere that also makes them freer. But we must also avoid that misuse of the Church's renewal that leads to betrayal, mockery, and desecration. Presumption and wrongdoing have always proved self-defeating in this world.

The Church is now in the midst of a great Advent period, a time of intense striving to prepare for the coming of the Lord. The Church wants to prepare itself far better than it has ever been prepared in the past. We know that this Advent period cannot mean just quiet waiting with our hands in our laps. Now is the moment for self-sacrifice, a time to prepare ourselves to love to the uttermost. If we are truly ready, the Lord will come into this world and give it peace. But the coming of the Lord will also show whether the world has closed itself to love and despised it; it will show whether people are only concerned for their own selves. Advent is the time of hope and also the time of decision. Both together. The coming of the Lord will show just how much we have believed in his life.

15. The Dialogue of Faith

The Church exists today between hope and fear. Some people are full of hope because they anticipate a fulfillment of their human existence from the developments that are taking place in the Church today. Other people anticipate the future with great fear because they see their own highest hopes threatened. The hopes of some and the fears of others have led to many discussions. There is a great dialogue going on today in the press, in the pulpit, in books, in private discussions, and in large public conferences. Ours is an age of "aggressive questioning," says Pope Paul. We are hearing unconventional and shocking opinions. On all sides, questions hit us with such force that "we cannot presuppose anything as believed or accepted. . . . We are forced to begin with the most elementary affirmations all over again." This is certainly the experience of many.

It is conceivable that many faithful people will feel themselves threatened by this vigorous discussion, criticism, doubt, and skepticism. But Pope Paul expressly demands of us that we think through "this aggressive questioning" and that we "find some answer to give." To neglect this dialogue says Pope Paul, would have "catastrophic consequences." We must enter into this great debate with confidence. It is a conversation between the Church and the world, a discussion among the many Christian churches, and a debate within the Catholic church itself. Why is this great dialogue so necessary to the life of the Church today?

Between the Church and the World

The desire for a conversation between the Church and the world was expressed by the Second Vatican Council, for the following reason: the Church should be the yeast, salt, and light of the world. But that can only occur when the Church stands in a living relation to the world. The Church does not exist for itself and does not exist to save its own life. The Church is like the yeast that exists only to leaven the bread.

The conversation between the Church and the world is more urgent in our day than in past centuries because the development of the world today is so rapid. The knowledge gained by history, psychology, and sociology poses many new questions, including new questions for religion. If we don't deal with these questions, then we will disappoint the peoples of the world. We are then responsible if they look for answers elsewhere.

The natural sciences have, for several centuries, also developed new methods of gaining knowledge. Technological man lives in terms of his experimentally gained knowledge. Contemporary man has quite different expectations in the religious realm than did the people who lived quietly on farms during past ages. Science brings many new questions. If we don't deal with these questions and expectations, then we ourselves will be guilty if technologically oriented people don't find their way to God and the Church, but are lost in confusion.

Between the Churches

The recent council also gave another reason why a great conversation is necessary today. Pope John XXIII called the bishops of the entire world to Rome and also invited the representatives of all other Christian churches. John's deathbed prayer was "that they all might be one." Pope John repeated with these words the prayer of Jesus Christ shortly before he died: that his disciples might all be one. "Father, let them all be one as you and I are one."

The coming together of Christian churches is a matter of greatest necessity in our time. We Christians are experiencing "the phenomenon of atheism, which is increasingly influencing people today—not only in those states where it is officially sanctioned, but also in that part of the world which once thought of itself as Christian and faithful." In the face of this increase of atheism in the world, Christians really have no other option but to come together and begin to discuss among themselves. We can no longer afford the luxury of division. This is another reason why the great debate among churches is so necessary today, and why it is not limited to discussions among professors of theology who write in scholarly journals. The debate has long since colored the thought of our age and is evidenced in the press, in magazines, in books, discussions, and sermons. That we have not yet found adequate solutions to these problems may cause some anxiety, but the situation has become unavoidable.

The Example of Christ

We cannot expect that this great conversation, that began with the Second Vatican Council, can be carried through in just a few months. The Eastern Orthodox churches, whose teachings are so close to our own, have been separated from us and gone their own way for a thousand years. How could we rearrange everything between us in just a few months? How can we understand one another by tomorrow when we have gone separate ways for a thousand years? There must be patience. The same thing holds true for discussions with our Protestant brothers and sisters. For about 150 years now, there has been a very stormy development of thought within Protestantism. Are we supposed to be able to immediately rethink and grasp all that has happened in Protestantism over 150 years? It is much the same, too, with our discussion with the world. At least since the time of the Enlightenment, in the eighteenth century, there have emerged many new ideas; many new ways of asking questions have popped up. We simply haven't worked all these things through yet. So our discussions with the world also require time. We need, therefore, patience and trust. But if God has created all persons in his image, so that we are his sons and daughters, then shouldn't we have the courage and confidence to talk together and try together to find the fullness of God's truth?

But there are many who are afraid. They fear that this great conversation will end in a fiasco. They know about the spirits of the world; they believe in those prophetic words which are written in the Apocalypse, the Book of Revelation. They expect little or nothing from such discussions—perhaps even harm. But Jesus Christ has given us a great example. When anything was necessary, then he did it. Even if it was dangerous—even when it might cost him his life—he did it. That was the attitude of his love for mankind. In the same way, we should believe this great conversation is necessary today, even though we are aware of its dangers. We owe it to the people of the world that we enter into this discussion in the spirit of love that Jesus Christ has taught to us.

Moreover, we do not want to be petty, for in the course of this conversation things will be hard enough. To chop down a tree means some chips have to fly. Wherever there is real hard thinking, there is also bound to be some error. If every single word has to be checked and pass examination—or if every attempt to make some progress gets judged and rejected—then the entire dialogue will get strangled before it has even begun. In this moment of the great conversation, we should concede the right of open speech to one another; we should grant people the right to their honest opinions, even if those opinions offend and rub us the wrong way.

Unity in All Things Necessary

But we also will say: we have our own convictions and we will not give them up. We will hold fast to our faith. We want to act in accordance with the Apostles' teaching: "Test all things; maintain those that are good." We wonder, therefore, where we shall be able to find a basis of intellectual cooperation and spiritual community among our debate partners? Is there some road that will bring us together? A road that is consistent with what each of us believes, so that neither of us is required to give up his convictions? The answer must be: we will not give up anything frivolously, and we will not accept new points of view just because they are interesting and fashionable. We will accept no revolutionary ideas just because they "swing." We will give up nothing that belongs to the essence or conditions of our faith.

But, in the course of this great conversation, we will reconsider with ever greater urgency what the teaching of the historical church documents really is. All the traditional teachings of the Church have been formulated as answers to questions that were asked in very specific historical circumstances. They were influenced by specific social and philosophical outlooks; they were all expressed in relation to certain historical presuppositions. The official explanations of the Church's teaching have never taken place in "pure and disinterested circumstances." Rather, the Church's explanation of its teaching has inevitably been mixed up with historically conditioned circumstances.

The great task of the debate today is to lift up the "permanent essence" of Christianity which is contained in the traditional explanations that have been put forth by the teaching office of the Church. This "permanent essence" can only be understood by us today *within our own historical circumstances.* That is, we will not be able to extract it in an historical way under "pure and disinterested circumstances." For the word of God has become flesh and ever since has presented itself to us in a very human way.

We do not expect a perfect unity in all things to result from this great conversation. All human knowledge is limited and every person sees life from a specific point of view. The goal of the dialogue is not unity down to the last jot and tittle. Rather, the goal is *unity in all things necessary.* Wherever we ourselves don't know how to conceive the word of God, we may and must maintain freedom. There must be unity in whatever is necessary, but freedom in whatever is doubtful.

Of course, we shall encounter opinions with which we, as faithful Christians, simply cannot agree. We will have to say exactly what it is that we cannot accept. Just the same, we will not judge any man nor throw anyone out the door. God alone knows the hearts of men. He alone has the judgment. We will judge no man, but we can say what the Church is and what it is not, what faith is and what faith is not.

The Lord of Dialogue

The heaviest weight of deciding what the Church and faith are (and what they are not) will be borne by the bishops and the teaching office of the Church. All the faithful rightly expect that the bishops will take part in this great conversation. But this must not mean that the bishops should make all the decisions by themselves. That would be impossible. Since the council, the bishops no longer are set apart. Just as the pope today works in closest cooperation with the bishops, the bishops are also required to work in close cooperation with theologians, priests, and the laity. The bishops will make their decisions only in cooperation with theological commissions, pastoral commissions, committees of priests, etc. Such groups already exist and are supported and utilized by the bishops in the exercise of their teaching office.

This great conversation between the churches, between the Church and the world, and within the Catholic church itself will not go on forever. It will be more like the reform of the Eucharist, a reform that is now coming to its conclusion. This does not mean that our thinking and wanting something better will not continue, but it does mean that our efforts to reconstruct do achieve specific results, as, for example, in the reform of the liturgy. The same thing holds true of the great dialogue. This conversation will not go on like some interminable experiment, but will come to a point of conclusion—like the reconstruction of a house. This does not mean that no further discussion will take place. It means, rather, that a part of the discussion will conclude by achieving definite results. We hope that all the faithful will be as satisfied with the results of this great debate as they have been with the reform of the Eucharist. Until that time, we need to have patience and give ourselves fully to this task.

The Church is initiating and guiding this great debate so that there may be a new unity. But the true initiator and leader of the dialogue must be God himself. If God is not there, then the debate will lack life and will have no chance of success or fruitfulness. Therefore, every Christian should contribute to this conversation so that God will be present in it. Our own conversation with God means that the great conversation of the Church can be successful. This great conversation with God can take place only in prayer. Our whole life must be a great conversation with God. The journey of our lives must be traveled with God. If God himself is a part of this great conversation of the Church, then we dare to have hope.

16. Dangers to Faith

The Second Vatican Council came as a surprise to all of us. In the discussion that took place between the time it was announced and its actual convocation, one frequently heard people say that this gathering would differ from those earlier councils which were called primarily to combat heresies. "Heresies," some said, "are a thing of the past. One doesn't really see—or at least pay attention to—heresy today." That's how we saw matters only a few years ago.

A Flight from Faith

Today, however, we would probably be a bit more cautious in making this kind of judgment. We might not call what we are experiencing today "heresy," for we are somewhat more restrained in using such strong words. But we are in the midst of a troublesome, uncertain, and confusing ferment: the crisis of authority, difficulties in adaptation, confusion and destruction of certain things (perhaps we might better call them "healing disorders"). This ferment can even lead to a flight from faith, to a flight from the things that are universally required into religious busywork, humanism, and revolution. Such things lead some to speak somewhat sadly about a "flight from the Church." Other people see in these things an occasion for rejoicing. They feel that the Church, which assumed that it would persist through all ages, is now creeping out of its protective bunker, and its eventual destruction is but a matter of time.

Should we blame the council for this situation? Has the council created the present situation of the Church? Was the council an error or a misjudgment? Perhaps even a heresy itself? Should we quickly reverse ourselves and declare the council, including all its teachings, to be annulled? Should we go back to the methods of past days—routing out heresy with fire and sword?

To these questions, we can answer clearly and boldly: No. If we analyze the present situation of the Church, even admitting its many mistakes and withdrawals, we still can answer no. The council is not to blame, because there was need to hold the council. The decisions of the council were good, even if they don't cover everything. Even ecclesiastical assemblies are not always perfect. The things the council decided upon are not bad. These decisions are not the problem, nor are the acts that carry them through; rather, the problem results from excesses and from cases of rigid one-sidedness.

For example, some people in the pursuit of reforms that are both right and necessary sometimes retreat too far from the central issues of faith. One can retreat by being concerned about many good and useful things instead of the one necessary thing, forgetting thereby the centrality of faith. The center of all things is personal faith. That is the one necessary thing that cannot be replaced by anything else. It is faith in God and in Jesus Christ, his Son; faith in the God-become-man and the man-become-God; faith in the Church, the sacraments, and the order established by Christ, for the sake of witnessing to him.

This flight from the center of faith is not the fault of the council. The pope, who knows that he is responsible for the whole Church, and who has expressed his concern in ever stronger words, is *a man of the council.* If the greatness of a man consists in being able both to break new roads and also to oppose those things

Leadership

that threaten danger, then Paul VI is a great pope. In his repeated statements opposing destructive tendencies in the Church today, Paul is not attempting to reestablish the older tradition of authority. Rather, he is concerned to further the reform, opening-up, and progress of the Church in the way pointed out by the council. But he sees this progress threatened on all sides by those who want to turn Church reform into a "permanent revolution," by those who want to make the Church's opening-up into the Church's dissolution. The pope is not striving to reinstate the old conditions in the Church, but to encourage it in its new way. He is not concerned with the past, but with the future. The things we are in danger of losing are not things that lie behind us, but things that still lie ahead.

The Multiplication Factor

Before turning to a discussion of specific things that might be regarded as "flights from the center of faith," it should be stated that every age always believes that it is living through the "decisive transition in the history of mankind." That is no less true today. And our age is just as important as every age before us and every age to come. But there is one thing that is special about our time, distinguishing it from earlier moments of history: the "democratic multiplication factor."

Many of the things that are dangers today were also dangers in earlier times: for example, the use of drugs or rampant, uncontrolled sexuality. But the problems these created in earlier times were not so great. These problems become real dangers today because they threaten to engulf whole masses of people. It is like this in the realms of faith and the Church. Many of today's problems existed earlier: the influence of secular ideas on theology, conflicting theological opinions, criticism of the external forms of Church structure, doubt about many of its teachings. But in earlier times, these things all remained confined to a somewhat narrow circle of people. The entirety of the Catholic community was not touched or disturbed by them.

Today, on the other hand, there are no longer any small or closed circles of discussion. Everything today seems of interest to everyone. The mass media believe it is their task to communicate every little thing, every statement of the pope as well as the personal opinion of every theologian. Whether it involves the important resolutions of a large official group or the private attitudes of some individual (e.g., the attitudes towards marriage of some college chaplain), all is communicated and treated in the same way. The only criterion is that something be "interesting." In fact, the mass media even try to make things "interesting" by popularizing and oversimplifying them, and by shifting their accent or tendency in order to make them more sensational. But what is sensational is never the normal, natural, understandable, and calm thing; rather it is the opposite. The sensational is the deviant, the unnatural, the argumentative, and loud thing. Hence, in order for something to win attention today, it must dress itself in the bright colors and shrill noises of SENSATION. In order for it to hold attention, it must exaggerate and be overformulated. And, most importantly, one must always seem to be *against something.* Against tradition. Against authority. Against received teaching. Against conventional morality.

For the most part, this does not happen because of

any bad will or sheer desire to be destructive. Rather, it happens because this is the way that the media operate today—even the Catholic media. It isn't the "bad theologians" who are trying to become good journalists in order to "sell" their ideas better. We shouldn't complain about this. And a widespread public interest in the Church is a good thing and is certainly better than a general indifference which finds anything having to do with the Church and faith completely uninteresting. We can be thankful for this interest in the Church without having to approve every form that this interest takes today.

Misunderstandings

The mass media, in what they select and discuss as "newsworthy," operate with a certain out-of-date view of the Church. This may not be their fault alone. It may, rather, simply show how much the Church and Catholics generally have failed to communicate their new self-understanding. In any case, the press, radio, and television all measure contemporary movements in the Church in the light of an image of some "nineteenth-century church" they have in the back of their minds. For them the Church is always a monolithic bloc; or, at least they pretend they think of the Church this way. But the Church has never been such a monolithic institution even though it may have liked to think of itself as such. There have always been tensions in the Church. However, when tensions in the Church appear today, the mass media presents them as if the Church were beginning to decay.

Moreover, the mass media always approach the world from a political point of view. This means that the media find politics everywhere and use political categories to describe what is going on. So, for example, the media see political "factions" in the Church; they describe these factions as "left" or "right," "progressive" or "conservative." Catholics themselves begin to utilize such terminology without really asking themselves whether they are at all adequate.

The mass media also judge the Church in terms of its most external manifestations. This, too, may not be the fault of the media alone. However, it means that when the media see changes in the outer form of the Church, they believe these mean changes in the Church itself. The change of temporally conditioned practices of the Church are then judged by the media to mean a desertion of the Church—in fact, the end of the Church. Many Catholics even think the same thing, which is not surprising since we are all children of our own age and think in its categories. And there are many other Catholics who think that everything wrong in the Church comes from the older forms of the Church and that salvation comes from the introduction of new practices.

Of course life requires constant change, the putting aside of familiar practices and conventions. In this sense, there is always a setting aside certain external forms that mediate the life of the Church. The Church of the nineteenth century is not our Church today, and our Church today will not be the Church of the twenty-first century—at least in its outward forms. Structures and external forms are but the clothes that the Church wears. Such clothes must be changed; the external practices must become different. But change is never created by talk alone.

A Flood of Words

Never before has there been so much discussion and so much writing as there is in the Church today. There is no longer any unquestioning authority; there is no longer any untouchable taboo. It is as if a long pent-up flood of words suddenly broke out and spilled over the whole Church. The danger here is less in the destruction a mere flood of words can do than in what this flood leaves behind: brackish water, putrid mud. The first critical words heard in synods or in the Catholic press were perhaps bold and freeing actions. But today the consciously intended provocation is no longer sensational. Nothing tires people quicker than to listen to endless talk. Perhaps it is time, therefore, to dam up the flood of words—not for so long that the dam will break again, but in such a way that our words can win new strength and become transformed into energy. That would happen if we could find some kind of orderly way to let them flow forth. We could turn the flood of words into a stream that would be focused and would create energy.

It appears that we are talking and writing too much today and that we're thinking and acting too little. Above all, we are praying too little. Prayer doesn't mean learning certain formulas by heart and then mechanically repeating them. Prayer means keeping oneself always open to God. For many people, to stress the importance of personal prayer is not a modern, but a nineteenth-century concern. They regard personal prayer as pietism, religious egotism, something dead and done with. Our age is more attuned to dialogue, to conversation with other people. But those who want such dialogue often forget that the model for talking with another person is, first of all, our dialogue with God. Prayer means talking with God. I can talk with my fellowman because I can talk with God. My respect for him as a brother, a "Thou" with whom I can speak, is secured and given dignity by my speaking to God and calling him "Thou." I speak with God not only in the common prayer of the liturgy, but also and most importantly, *alone.* Faith has a social dimension, but *not only a social dimension.* Faith is, first of all, an inward personal relation between man and God. We must not forget this.

To stress this heart of faith does not mean a denial of the things we are seeking to accomplish in reforming the Church. Quite the contrary. In order to renew the Church, we must be careful that our new proposals not lose their relationship with the heart of faith. The new can only be effective if it is always tied to the personal faith of individual believers. Then renewal will not be a flight from faith, but something that will endure.

Discerning the Spirits

The Church is made up of people and these people think in terms of the categories and forms appropriate to their age. The Church will also share in the errors of the age in which it lives. The promised gift of the Holy Spirit does not mean that the members of the Church are protected from error, but that the Church—in all directions and misdirections—will always find its way to truth, faith, hope, and love.

Every way can be a false way when it becomes absolutized. The ways of our day are called rationalism, empiricism, criticism, and the "democratic way of life." It would be nonsense to attempt to abolish the spirit of our age which manifests itself in all these different movements. But it would be fateful if we failed to see the temporally conditioned character of the modern age, if we failed to see its limitations. It would be tragic were we to accept this modern age unconditionally, accept it as true precisely at those points where it overstepped its own limits.

This holds true, also, within the Church. There can be no technical progress without empiricism and rationalization. God gave reason to man so that he could use it—even use it in religion. All the elements of religion that can be illuminated by reason should be so illuminated. All the things that must be demythologized should be demythologized. But reason begins to contradict itself when it believes that everything in the realm of religion can be explained logically and rationally. At the heart of all religion there is a dimension of mystery that is not accessible to reason. Religion that has no mystery, no secret, is not religion. Perhaps it is a social ethic. Every religion should be at least this. But if it is no more than this, then it will never be able to answer our ultimate question—no matter how many other questions it can answer. These ultimate questions are: "Where do I come from; where am I going; why am I in the world?"

Questions like these are asked by individual persons. Individual persons want answers for themselves. Human beings are, of course, social beings. We know this better today than we did in the past. We see more sharply today the consequences of egotism in business and society, an egotism about one's class, or race, or people. There is also a religious egotism that thinks only about its own salvation, that wants only to save its own soul while remaining blind and deaf to the needs of other men and women. We see the social function of religion more clearly today than we did in the past.

But man is not only a social being. Man is no one-dimensional being. He lives, rather, in dimensions of life that are distinct, and even opposed. Man exists in a state of tension; some of his acts contradict others. Wherever this tension is lacking, life is extinguished. From the point of view of sheer social structure, termites and bees are more thoroughly organized. There is a long-standing fantasy among men that they might build a state that would function as efficiently as an ant colony—reproducing only as many new lives as the state needed, and genetically controlling this new life so that it would fulfill its social function.

So far all such attempts have not succeeded. Man is easily manipulable; but there is some residual part of him that is not transformable. In spite of all efforts, there is always a human residue remaining. There is always a question remaining. As long as man cannot be weaned from this question, he will remain a human being—and not become an exchangeable number. A human being will always ask questions about his origins, his future, and the meaning of his existence. And he will not let himself be satisfied with the notion that everything comes from matter that is eternal. You are nothing; matter is all. You are nothing; your race, class, or people are all.

Man refuses to be *nothing;* he refuses to be a number, a mere function. He wants to be a person. He wants to hear a personal answer to his personal questioning. He feels himself to be a unique, and not a repeatable, exchangeable thing. He wants an answer that in some way respects him as a person. Only religion can give him this answer. It cannot be given him in mathematical formulas, philosophical teachings, or scientific definitions. It can only be given to him in images and parables, in myth and revelation. For this reason, man will always shatter specific historical forms. He can always destroy them. But he can never dissolve faith itself. The historical form of religion can pass away with an age; but religion itself is indestructible.

It seems necessary to say this since there are many people today who believe that Christianity could save itself if it would abandon its religious language and paraphernalia. They want to create a religionless Christianity, a demythologized and immanentist version of the Christian faith. They want this because they believe that religion is an historically conditioned phenomenon that will pass away in time. They want this because they feel that the Christianity to which they adhere can only survive when purified from everything mythological, religious, and transcendent.

The proposal to create a religionless Christianity is one more flight from faith. Certainly it is not undertaken out of hatred, disinterest, or discontentment. Quite the contrary. It is undertaken out of the mistaken opinion that Christian faith can only be saved if one denies that it is a religion. Atheism is not what motivates such a proposal. But atheism will follow as its consequence.

Building Faith in Our Time

In this context, we must now ask exactly what faith today is—and how faith presents itself to the believer.

Our faith today is not triumphalist, victorious, or the shining testimony of unshaken certainty. Rather, our faith today is more like the faith of the man in the gospels who wanted to be healed: "Lord, I believe; help my unbelief." For many people today, faith is first of all "wanting to believe." Its force comes from the heart rather than from the head. Logical proofs for God are not really what are sought.

But to be able to believe, a person must also pray—however contradictory this may seem to be. For many persons, faith today does not mean being lifted up to the bright heights; rather, it means stumbling and feeling one's way through the night of darkness—through the emptiness, the doubt, the absence of God. This night is only illuminated by the tender flame of hope and trust in God's word. This trust cannot overcome the doubt, but it can give us the courage to doubt the doubt.

Faith was never easy. Even a brief study of the lives of the saints teaches us that. Faith can never presume to know better or to be something exclusive. Rather, faith is modest and thankful, always needing help, always susceptible to difficulties. But faith is hopeful; again and again faith is hopeful. It hopes in the help that it needs. "Lord, I believe; help my unbelief."

We can help faith if we will complete the renewal of the liturgy so that it becomes more understandable. But we create difficulties for faith if we dig up new experiments for every service. The destruction of religion begins with the destruction of the services of worship, the liturgy.

We can also strengthen faith by scholarly research if we distinguish the enduring heart of religion from its temporally conditioned expressions. But we can disturb and even destroy faith if sociology overextends its conceptual boundaries so that people begin to believe that the actual forms of behavior are the only forms of behavior that ought to exist. To say we should do something because other people are doing it is simply an absurdity.

We can strengthen faith if we intellectually clarify what in religion is accessible to reason. But we can disturb and even destroy faith if we believe that we must exhaustively explain every mystery and every myth that is part of religion. Theology is an intellectual discipline, even a "science." But religion is more than that. A religion that meets every scientific test is no longer a religion. Whatever can be completely grasped by human understanding certainly leaves no room for divine revelation.

We can strengthen faith if we point out its social obligations. But we can only disturb and destroy it if we believe that faith can only express itself through social involvement. Social involvement is no substitute for religion. Adaptation to the world can never replace openness to God. The social function is not the only function of faith.

We can certainly also aid faith by approaching things critically, including even the true and proper authorities within the Church. Every human authority must be questioned and confronted with the highest authority of all, the authority of God. We will only injure and destroy faith, however, if we do not oppose the view that there should be absolutely no authority in the Church. Even ecumenism—the striving for a unity in faith—can become a dangerous flight from faith if it leads to indifference about the truth. Or if it is a mere flight into organizational busywork.

Importance of the Church

Faith can also be strengthened by the changing of Church structures so that they are adapted to the needs of our time. But the future of faith certainly doesn't consist only in changing the structures of the Church. In fact, the zealous search for new Church structures can itself become just frantic activity which masks the flight from faith—unless that activity is grounded on a decision of personal faith by the individual.

Everything that strengthens the personal faith of the individual will also be helpful to the whole Church. Whatever endangers the personal faith of the individual will also endanger the faith of the whole Church. The Church does not exist in order to preach a new humanism. The Church is not a safe in which the treasures of human culture are stored and protected. It is also no stronghold of bourgeois values and conventions. And it is no outpost for preparing social revolution. The Church is not necessary for any of these things, even if there are those who want to misuse the Church by promoting them through it. The Church exists in order to teach and further faith in God, the Almighty Creator, and his son Jesus Christ, our Savior. The Church exists to preserve the sacraments that Jesus Christ established—the sacraments that are the outer form of the secret of religion and the mystery of faith. This faith, however, is always the personal decision of individuals. The believing community and its common worship can surely provide an important help and support for this personal decision. In fact, in many cases it plays the decisive role. But faith is always a personal decision made by an individual.

Everything that we want to make new within the

Church can only become effective if we connect it with personal faith. The foundation of "love your neighbor" is the commandment to "love God with all your heart and soul and might." A faith that is not manifested in the world is dead. But mere worldly concern without faith in God is only sound and fury, signifying nothing. Mere involvement in the world without love for God is not faith, but flight. Everything depends on a personal decision of faith.

75 10 9 8 7 6 5 4 3 2 1